European

gle market

This book is due for

EUROPEAN COMMISSION

Cataloguing data can be found at the end of this publication

This guide is an introduction to consumer affairs legislation in the European Union and to other measures designed to benefit consumers. As such, its purpose is to help consumers understand the complexities of the underlying law.

Consumers who have a personal legal problem are advised to consult the relevant legal texts and/or a lawyer.

Luxembourg: Office for Official Publications of the European Communities, 1996

ISBN 92-827-4859-6

Printed in Germany

Contents

Foreword by

Emma Bonino
Commissioner responsible for consumer policy

This Guide is the brainchild of Christiane Scrivener, my predecessor as Commissioner responsible for consumer policy in the European Union.

The objective is simple

The purpose of this guide is very down-to-earth — namely: to set out the plain facts on the European dimension of consumer protection. We want to give our readers the confidence necessary to explore the advantages of the single market and play a part in building it.

Easier said than done

The objective might seem simple but in the process we have run up against **two big obstacles.**

Firstly, **in institutional and political terms,** the European Union is somewhat remote from its citizens. In general, very few people have direct personal contacts with any of the Union institutions. Likewise, most Community-level laws take the shape of 'directives' which are addressed to the governments, which in turn must 'transpose' them into national law for them to take effect.

The result of this 'remoteness' and the complexities of law-making is to muddy the waters so that people end up believing that:

- **everything that is good comes from the national government and**
- **Brussels is at the root of all problems.**

I hope that this guide will give you a different perspective.

A second obstacle arises from the fact that any **decision taken at Community level is inevitably a compromise** between different viewpoints, both sectoral and national. Hence, nobody is completely happy and inconsistencies are liable to occur or indeed thorny problems may remain unresolved.

So, give us a hand...

Since this Guide in no way claims that 'all is for the best in the best of all possible worlds', each chapter deals with a number of fields in which future action at Community level might improve the consumer's lot.

If you agree with these points, or even if you have different ideas on the subject, let us know what you think. Likewise — since this Guide does not aspire to be an exhaustive inventory of the legislation in force — if you find deficiencies or shortcomings, don't hesitate to let us know. If the Single Market is to be **at your service**, you must **play your part in its construction** by voicing your criticisms and your preferences.

Introduction

 What? The single market affects me?

When:

- in your local supermarket, you are wondering whether to buy Parma ham or Ardennes ham, or

- you are looking for a toy for your child, or

- you suffer from angina and want to know whether the drugs your doctor has prescribed have side-effects,

you have other things on your mind than the European Union.

However, in these and similar everyday episodes we can see **the concrete impact of the European Union,** and more specifically the benefits of the single market.

Sadly, only a well-informed observer will be aware of this because these advantages are all too often overshadowed by the 'big political picture'.

This is why some people wrongly believe that the single market has no effect on their daily life. Hence this guide proposes a number of remedies to dispel these preconceptions.

 What can the single market mean for someone like me?

The essence of the single market may be summarized in two words: 'free movement'. By this we mean the unhindered movement of goods and services, individuals and capital between the now 15 countries of the European

Union as though it were a single country or a single market.

In practical terms this means two things:

- you will be faced with a wide range of products and services offered by firms from other countries;

- you yourself are quite free to do business with firms abroad.

Moreover, the completion of the single market, and more recently the celebrated 'Maastricht Treaty', gives new rights to the citizens of the Union.

As a consumer in the single market, you have various **rights,** including:

- **the right to buy goods and services,** for private use, in another country of the Union, and to take them home with you without paying customs duties or supplementary taxes (with very few exceptions);

- **the right to transfer money** to another country, for example for current transactions or to make investments;

- **the right to borrow money** from a lender in another country of the Union.

 But don't I also have the right to work in another country and, if I live there, to have the vote, for example?

Correct! You have these rights and you may, for example:

- go and study in another Member State;

- benefit from the social security system of another Member State just like local residents;

- obtain urgent health care, when abroad, on the same terms as the local residents;

- live in another Member State as a worker or self-employed person, pensioner or student;

- vote in local elections or in elections to the European Parliament.

 So this guide is going to explain all these rights in detail?

No! To do so would make it too long and boring.

Firstly, **this guide concerns you only in your capacity as a 'consumer'.** So you won't find answers to work-related questions, such as problems concerning the recognition of diplomas or your social security rights.

Secondly, this guide is conceived first and foremost as a **practical introduction to the single market** and not as an exhaustive repertory of the legislation in force. It looks at areas in which the European Union has taken measures to protect consumers, but steers clear of irrelevant detail because the situation is evolving from day to day.

The idea here is to introduce you **to the new opportunities offered by the single market** and to encourage you, if you are interested, to explore them.

 Great stuff ... but the problem is I've always found it hard to follow your Eurocrat jargon

Don't worry! You're not the only one — and it is precisely for people like you that this guide has been designed.

We've tried to translate the legal jargon **into plain language in a way we hope everyone will understand.**

The average consumer is mainly interested in the practical effect of the law and normally has no inclination to linger over the small print. So, wherever possible, this guide steers clear of the procedures and language of the law.

However, if you want to learn a bit more about the legal side, you will find in Annex B:

- a brief description of the institutions of the European Union;

- an explanation of the different types of Community legal instruments.

 Fine! This is getting interesting but what will I find in this guide?

As we have already mentioned, the presentation is in **the form of dialogues** explaining how the single market established by the European Union **protects your physical well being, safeguards your economic interests and endows you with rights** while offering you **a better choice at competitive prices.**

You can read this guide either from start to finish or dip into it with the aid of the Contents page.

Briefly, the next three chapters investigate **shopping abroad** and related issues such as VAT and how to get information and advice about cross-border transactions.

However, you don't have to leave your own country to enjoy the benefits of the single market. On the contrary, for most consumers **the single market already exists.** Hence the guide continues with a section devoted to **general topics** such as general product safety or advertising and then goes on to tackle **specific sectors,** such as foodstuffs and package holidays.

Each chapter also contains **some useful advice** and a review of **certain aspects of consumer protection which need to be reinforced.**

PART I

Cross-border shopping

1. Shopping abroad

Shopping abroad — no problem?

Buying a camera abroad, filling the boot with wine or food-stuffs abroad, buying a flat or investing money abroad — this will soon be an everyday occurrence.

To make the most of the single market, consumers must be sure that their interests are protected. So they need objective information, a clear legislative framework and possibly even legal assistance.

However, the single market, being of recent vintage, is synonymous both with common rules on quality, safety and health and, in the legal domain, with greater risks.

This chapter surveys what has been done to enable consumers to benefit from the single market. Specific sectors are dealt with in greater detail in other chapters of this guide.

I never thought of shopping abroad on a big scale — what's in it for me?

Price, quality and choice are the three main criteria that motivate people to look abroad for bargains.

Better prices! Obviously, the first motive is to save money. For certain goods and services, the differences in prices between countries make it worth shopping around.

Quality! This is another key point that would seem to explain why there is so much cross-border trade in certain regions.

Choice! This third element is a big factor because, even today, you will not always find exactly what you need locally. Elsewhere, though, you can stock up on aperitifs or wines, or have an enormous range of cassettes, discs, toys, etc. to choose from.

 But what do our neighbours have that is so interesting?

Staple consumer goods — drinks and foodstuffs, as well as clothing and footwear — are highly prized. However, consumer durables are the poor relations in cross-border trade. Probably this is because of the lack of harmonization in technical standards (sockets being the best example) and fears of potential servicing or warranty problems.

Products and services that sell well vary from country to country. Here are some examples:

■ **Denmark** for furniture;

■ in **Germany**, the favourites are household appliances, cameras, cars, banking services, insurance, medicines, furniture and foodstuffs;

■ in **Spain**, wine is very sought after;

- in **France**, wine, foodstuffs, pharmaceutical products, cars and package holidays;

- **Italy** is renowned for the quality of its clothes, wines, furniture and food;

- **Luxembourg** has very competitive fuel prices and banking services;

- **Sweden's** glass and crystal goods are much sought after by connoisseurs;

- finally, the **United Kingdom** has a good reputation for insurance and medicines.

Sounds interesting — but where's the snag?

Naturally you can't expect shopping abroad to become as easy overnight as shopping round the corner.

The **main problems** are as follows:

- The language barrier: unless you're a polyglot, it may be difficult to communicate with a supplier, manufacturer or consumer organization in another country. The language problem also arises in figuring out legal texts, which are often drafted solely in the language of the country of sale.

- Lack of information: information on the range of products offered, the prices, terms of sale, and where to turn in the event of problems, is not always readily available.

- The different standards: standards governing consumer health and safety still differ somewhat, despite the endeavours of the European Union to ensure that products on sale abroad are just as safe as those manufactured or sold at home.

- The different legal systems: ignorance of the applicable law and the complexity of what is known as 'international private law' are very dissuasive factors. The law applicable to the 'substance' of a dispute and the law applicable to the 'procedure' which allows you to exercise your rights depend on a host of international rules and conventions whose operation is quite complex. Even if the court in your country has jurisdiction over a dispute, it may be difficult to enforce its decision against a firm based in another country. However, between the Member States of the European Union, the formalities governing the jurisdiction and enforcement of judgments in civil and commercial matters have been simplified through a Community convention called the 'Brussels Convention'.

- Payment for purchases made abroad: plastic money and cheques are not accepted on the same terms in all countries. In some cases stores prefer cash payment or Eurocheques.

- Guarantees and after-sales services: suppliers rarely offer a warranty that is valid throughout the European Union. Hence, if a defect occurs it is not always easy to have the item repaired or exchanged on reasonable terms.

 This looks like being a real headache. Hasn't the European Union done anything to make things easier for consumers?

But of course! It goes without saying that the single market cannot succeed **without active and confident consumer participation.** So the European Union has earmarked some of its resources to protecting consumers' interests, with a view to:

- encouraging better information;

- establishing a statutory framework;

- facilitating access to justice.

Fine, but tell me more about the legal framework, for a start.

The European Community has put a lot of effort into **harmonizing laws to establish an identical level of protection in all countries.** The Community has adopted a range of texts designed to increase your protection and facilitate cross-border trade. Examples include:

- general product safety;

- manufacturers' liability/liability for defective products;

- dangerous imitations;

- toy safety;

- cosmetic products;

- textile names;

- package travel, package holidays and package tours;

- labelling and presentation of foodstuffs intended for the final consumer and advertising in this regard;

- misleading advertising;

- indication of prices of foodstuffs and non-food products;

- unfair terms in consumer contracts;

- contracts negotiated at a distance;

- contracts negotiated away from business premises;

- the purchase of the right to use immovable properties on a timeshare basis;

- consumer credit;

- payment systems and in particular relations between cardholders and card issuers.

More detailed information is to be found in the following chapters.

 Then, what about the lack of information?

The European Union has been closely involved in the creation of **centres for information and advice on cross-border purchases**. These are mainly intended for people in frontier regions, but all consumers may consult them. They provide useful information in several languages and employ multilingual staff (see Chapter 3).

The European Union is also encouraging consumer associations to expand their programmes of **comparative tests** so that the published results will reflect the new realities of the single market (for example, by providing information on the range of models — along with prices — for sale in neighbouring countries, and not only on the situation in one country).

The Union is also active in improving the information on **product labels.**

Finally, don't forget that this **guide** itself is also a way of learning more about the single market.

 ... and what about the distance factor?

Although there is no way of reducing physical distances as such, many of the obstacles can be overcome through such expedients as **distance selling**. This selling technique has always been popular in the form of mail-order purchases and, more recently, tele-shopping has come into vogue. Since some of these variants are likely to expand rapidly in the years to come, and since national laws governing them are different, the European Union has prepared legislation on 'contracts negotiated at a distance'. This legislation governs several varieties of transactions of this kind, including tele-shopping! (See Chapter 6.)

Don't forget either that all Community initiatives designed to improve transport and telecommunications will benefit consumers as well as business. For example, consider the changes brought about by motorways, high-speed trains and, just recently, the Channel Tunnel — indeed we now have an embarrassment of facilities to tempt people to shop abroad!

 ### *... and the different standards?*

The Community is doing its utmost to ensure that consumers in all Member States enjoy the same level of protection. A certain number of minimum standards have been introduced with regard to consumer health and safety. This is necessary to put into practice:

- **specific legislation on certain products** (see for example Chapters 11, 12 and 13 on pharmaceutical products, cosmetic products and toys);

- **legislation on general product safety** (see Chapter 4);

- certain **measures concerning foodstuffs** (see Chapter 10).

 ### *... and paying for my purchases abroad?*

You are entitled to take with you whatever money you need to pay for your purchases, or to transfer the money to another country of the Union.

Consult your bank for information on the various modes of payment that already exist (cash, payment card or credit card, Eurocheque, etc.) and don't forget to ask for details on charges and how long it takes for the money to arrive.

Careful! Bank charges for transferring small sums may be relatively high, although some financial institutions are currently lowering their tariffs. **First, get the information you need** and don't forget that the **post offices** have their own system of international transfers which is often cheaper than the banks for small sums.

For more details on financial services, consult Chapter 18.

...and guarantees?

At Community level the Commission is looking into various ways of harmonizing conditions pertaining to guarantees and after-sales service. The proposals have been published in a Green Paper designed to elicit feedback from interested parties.

Pending possible Community legislation, **the question of guarantees is still governed by national rules.**

Generally, the seller is liable for the commercial or legal guarantee. In certain cases the manufacturer may offer his own warranty, but he is not obliged to do so.

... and legal redress?

As you can imagine, settling a dispute with a supplier based in another country may prove far from straightforward.

A number of 'pilot schemes' for the smoother handling of consumer disputes have been launched, thanks in part to the support of the Commission, which has begun to legislate in this field.

Some hints

Reading this guide will make you more aware as a consumer. Remember that many problems can be avoided if you take a little bit of trouble at the right time.

So, look before you leap. This applies particularly if you intend to spend a considerable sum. But even for your daily shopping, you can always check out the week's special offers.

Compare products and services. Examine all the information and compare quality, price, service, etc.

Assert your rights. If what you bought doesn't meet your expectations, or if you think your rights have been violated, tell the supplier and if necessary the authorities or a consumer association. You will get satisfaction more often than you might expect and your initiative may make life easier for other people in the future.

Become an active consumer. Joining a consumer association will give you access to regular information, including results of comparative tests, and may help you get more value for your money. Moreover, certain associations have a legal aid service, which may be invaluable in the event of problems.

What remains to be done

Much remains to be done, no doubt about that: certain Community proposals have yet to be adopted, studies have to be carried out, and solutions found to everyday or legal problems.

Even if certain firms already provide a warranty that is valid in all the Member States, you should remember that the scope and content of this warranty may vary from one country to another. Unfortunately, there is still no Community text governing guarantee conditions and after-sales services. But a Green Paper containing proposals in this domain has been distributed to elicit feedback from both suppliers and consumers.

Likewise, as regards the options described in the Green Paper on access to justice, the consultation process has not yet been concluded, and a decision as to the appropriate measures has yet to be taken.

The establishment of monetary union, with a single currency, will eliminate charges associated with buying foreign currency and will facilitate payments throughout the Community.

When are the shops open?

NB: The situation varies considerably from one country to another, and even from region to region within individual countries.

■ The situation is most 'flexible' in **Portugal**, because shops can open at any time between 6 a.m. and midnight, provided they comply with the normal rules on the length of the working day.

■ There are no restrictions in **Ireland** but in practice the shops are open until 6 or 7 p.m. on weekdays and until 6 p.m. on Saturday; supermarkets remain open until 9 p.m. on Thursdays and Fridays. During December, shops may open on Sunday.

■ In other countries, such as **Germany, Denmark** and **Italy**, there is legislation governing shop opening hours, but there are many exemptions. In Denmark and Italy, this legislation is currently the subject of vigorous debate.

To be on the safe side you should get information on shop opening hours before you visit another Member State.

2. VAT

Goodbye to the tax frontiers

The internal market means first and foremost the free movement of goods and services. Consumers are free to shop
anywhere for products and services for their personal use.

Hence, since 1 January 1993 the European Community has
abolished most intra-Community border formalities. With the
exception of new motor vehicles (including motor cycles and
boats) and 'tax-free' purchases, you now pay VAT directly on
purchase. Hence the red tape associated with VAT is a thing
of the past. You are now completely free to transport purchases for personal use across the internal frontiers.

Since 1993, you have nothing to declare!

So, going through customs really has become easier?

Yes! Remember that a few years ago whenever you returned home from a trip abroad you had to stop at the border to declare your purchases. Over a certain value or for some products purchased in excess of a certain quantity you had to pay customs duty and VAT at the rate applicable in your country, after deduction of taxes paid in the country of purchase. **Hassle galore!**

Today, all this is history. Since 1 January 1993 customs officers are no longer concerned about the value or quantity of goods in your baggage — be it the latest camcorder, your favourite sherry or goodies for the children. **Provided, of course, that all these goods are intended for your personal use.**

 Does that mean that I can cross the internal borders with a lorryload of wine?

Don't let's get confused! The opening of borders is not a warrant to smuggle!

You may only transport merchandise for personal use. This means that in certain cases you have to justify your purchases. For example, let's say you have bought several freezers in Luxembourg to store vegetables from your large and very fertile garden. The customs officer, intrigued by the number of freezers you are transporting, may ask for an explanation. Then you will have to prove that you do not intend to sell these items but that they are intended for your personal use.

Customs officers may also begin to suspect that something is afoot and remind you of the rules if you are carrying more than:

- 800 cigarettes,

- 90 litres of wine,

- 110 litres of beer and

- 10 litres of spirits.

The officer may enquire how come you need all these products for your personal use. But if you explain to him that your daughter is getting married and that there will be a big party, and if you can justify it, you should not have any problem.

Beware! In four Member States **(Ireland, Denmark, Finland and Sweden)**, the authorities have been authorized to impose lower ceilings. **Irish** citizens are limited to 45 litres of wine and 55 litres of beer, the **Danes** to 300 cigarettes and 1.5 litres of alcohol (including the duty-free allowance, and even less if they have been out of Denmark for less than 36 hours!) and the **Finns** and **Swedes** to 1 litre of alcohol, 5 litres of wine and 15 litres of beer.

 So this means that I can go shopping anywhere just like at home?

Exactly. From now on, when — say — you buy a small TV set in the Netherlands, **you will simply pay the VAT,** included in the price at the local rate applicable in the Netherlands at the time of purchase, without any special invoice and without having to make complicated calculations.

 Great stuff! So let's go and buy a new car in Spain!

Beware! New motor cars, motor bikes and boats are the sole exception to the rule. They continue to be **taxed in your country of residence.**

If you prefer to buy a **second-hand car,** the taxes may be different or non-existent, depending on whether you purchase from a private party or through a dealer (see Chapter 15 on motor cars).

 At any rate, I've been told that the price of cars is about to fall.

Perfectly true! In Spain, Greece, Italy, Portugal, France and Belgium VAT on cars and other 'luxury' products has already been cut. Thus, **the most significant tax discrepan-**

cies between the countries of the Community have already disappeared.

The benefits are by no means negligible. The French Finance Ministry gives the example of a Renault Clio purchased for FF 52 000 in November 1993, which would have cost FF 58 000 if VAT had not been cut. However, your government may have slapped on a different tax, as is the case in Belgium.

 But what about 'duty-free' sales if there are no more borders?

A good question! If you are travelling within the EU, you are still entitled to buy 'duty-free' goods in airports and ports until **30 June 1999**.

After that date, duty-free shops will be restricted to travellers entering or leaving the Community. This means that you won't be able to do duty-free shopping if you're flying from Paris to Athens, for example.

Moreover, duty-free purchases are and will remain strictly regulated: **the quantities of products sold are limited per person and trip.**

Since 1 April 1994 the limits have been quadrupled for travellers **entering or leaving Community territory,** i.e. the maximum value of your duty-free purchases is now ECU 175 as opposed to ECU 45 in the past. This rule applies to all travellers aged over 15 (in Germany, Denmark and the United Kingdom it applies to all travellers, irrespective of age).

On the other hand, **if you are travelling within the Community,** the maximum value of your duty-free purchases is now ECU 90 as opposed to ECU 45 in the past.

In terms of quantity, the limits are:

- 200 cigarettes,

- 1 litre of alcoholic beverage,

- 50 grammes of perfume

for all travellers.

Distance selling: VAT is included here too!

Mail-order purchasers should know that from now on, when they place an order abroad, VAT will be included in the price and that the merchandise will be sent directly to their homes. There are no formalities to be completed, whether the purchases are made from a catalogue, by correspondence, or by teleshopping (see Chapter 6 on distance selling).

VAT generally applied in the Member States to certain products or services at 1 April 1995

Products and services	B	DK	D	GR	E	F	
Foodstuffs	6/12/20.5	25	7/15	8	4/7	5.5/18.6	
Drinks:							
– Alcohol, wine, beer	20.5	25	15	18	16	18.6	
– Mineral water, lemonade, fruit juice	20.5	25	15	8	7/16/7	5.5	
Clothing: Adults	20.5	25	15	18	16	18.6	
Children	20.5	25	15	18	16	18.6	
Footwear: Adults	20.5	25	15	18	16	18.6	
Children	20.5	25	15	18	16	18.6	
Pharmaceutical products	6	25	15	8	4	2.1/5.5	
Tobacco	20.5	25	15	18	16	18.6	
Books	6	25	7	4	4	5.5	
Daily newspapers	0	0	7	4	4	2.1	
Periodicals	0	25	7	4	4	2.1	
Hifi-video	20.5	25	15	18	16	18.6	
Household appliances	20.5	25	15	18	16	18.6	
Furs/jewellery	20.5	25	15	18	16	18.6	
Petrol	20.5	25	15	18	16	18.6	
Motor vehicles	20.5	25	15	18	16	18.6	
Personal transport: domestic	6	25/ exon.	7/15	8	7/16	5.5	
Hotels	6	25	15	8	7	5.5	
Restaurants	20.5	25	15	8/18	7	18.6	
Works of art	6	25	7	8	16/7 (marge)	5.5/18.6 (marge)	
Antiques	6	25	15	8	16/7 (marge)	5.5/18.6 (marge)	
Second-hand goods	(marge)	25	(marge)	8/18	16/7 (marge)	5.5/18.6 (marge)	
Travel agencies	20.5	exon.	15	18	16	18.6	
Cut flowers and plants:							
– decorative use	20.5	25	7	18	7	5.5	
– foodstuffs production	6/12	25	7	4/8	7	5.5	

IRL	I	L	NL	AT	P	FI	SE	UK
0/2.5/12.5/21	4/10/16	3	6	10	5/17	17	21	0
21	19/16/19	15/12/15	17.5	20/12-20 20	17/5/17	22	25	17.5
21	19	3	6	20	17	22	21	7.5
21	16	12/15	17.5	20	17	22	25	17.5
0	16	3	17.5	20	17	22	25	0
21	16	15	17.5	20	17	22	25	17.5
0	16	3	17.5	20	17	22	25	0
0/21	4	3	6	20	5	12	25	0
21	19	12	17.5	20	17	22	25	17.5
0	4	3	6	10	5	12	25	0
12.5	4	3	6	10	5	0/22	0	0
21	4	3	6	10	5	0/22	25	0
21	10/19	15	17.5	20	17	22	25	17.5
21	19	15	17.5	20	17	22	25	17.5
21	19	15	17.5	20	17	22	25	17.5
21	19	12/15	17.5	20	17	22	25	17.5
21	19	15	17.5	20	17	22	25	17.5
exon.	10/19/ exon.	3/ exon.	6/ exon.	10	5	6	12	0
12.5	10	3	6	10	5	6	12	17.5
12.5	10/19	3	6	10/20	17	22	25	17.5
12.5	19	6	6	10	17(marge)/exon.	22 (marge)	25	0/17.5 (marge)
12.5	19	15	6	10	17(marge)/exon.	22 (marge)	25	0/17.5 (marge)
0/21 (marge)	19/16/10	15	17.5	20	17 (marge)	22 (marge)	25	17.5 (marge)
exon.	19	12	exon.	20	17	22	25	17.5
21	19	3	6	10	17	22	25	17.5
0	16	3	6	10	5			0

3. Information, advice and access to justice

On becoming an informed consumer

Faced with an ever-growing range of products and services and ubiquitous advertising, you may easily feel out of your depth. However, given the economic and indeed social pressures, you, like most people, want to get best value for money by making judicious choices.

In such a situation, objective and reliable information is vital, together with disinterested expert advice of all kinds and, if a dispute becomes inevitable, ready access to justice.

As you will discover, a large number of organizations of all kinds — at local, regional, national and even Community level — have already been created and are there to provide you with on-the-spot assistance whenever you need it.

By making use of the different sources of information and advice and becoming an informed consumer, you will make enlightened choices, steer clear of pitfalls and ultimately be better placed to assert your rights.

It's not always easy for consumers to make the right choice. Where can I get information and advice?

Generally speaking there is no shortage of useful information — the problem is rather knowing where to find it.

In all countries of the European Union there are public and private institutions whose job is to help consumers. Since **structures and traditions differ greatly** from one country to another, and since many of the agencies are specialized in certain aspects of consumer affairs, it is difficult to indicate the right way to resolve a given problem.

However, no matter what nationality you are, your first reflex as an informed consumer should be to **contact a consumer organization.** You should know that:

- in certain countries (Germany for example), consumer organizations have high-street premises and a network of offices open to the public; in other countries (such as the Netherlands or the United Kingdom), you have to contact the central office;

- some organizations are active only at local or regional level (though often they are members of a wider federation), while others are active at national level; likewise, the range of services offered may vary;

- depending on the type of organization, **you may have to become a member.** And depending on the material you want to take away or have mailed to you (brochures, test reports, etc.), you may have to pay a fee.

Annex A to this guide contains a list of useful addresses, though it is by no means exhaustive. If the organization listed cannot answer your question, it may tell you who can, or direct you to an information source close to you.

Finally, there are yet other ways of becoming a well-informed consumer. For instance, **periodicals** published by consumer protection organizations are not always restricted to fee-paying members; some are on sale at your local newsagent. Moreover, programmes on controversial consumer issues are broadcast by various **radio and television stations** in Europe. Likewise, many journals and magazines have sections or even whole pages devoted to consumer problems. **But beware of surreptitious advertising** and sponsored broadcasts or supplements. **Rather, seek out neutral and objective information.**

 Agreed, but let's be more precise: how can I pinpoint the best products and services?

It is precisely to answer this question that a large number of consumer organizations publish the results of market and price **surveys.** The most familiar type of survey is the **comparative tests** conducted regularly by the large organizations, whose results are published in their magazines.

In certain regions there are **weekly price surveys** for different products and periodical comparisons of prices in the supermarkets, surveys on water quality, etc.

Generally, the purpose of such publications is to help you choose by providing useful advice. This means that before purchasing a camera, a vacuum cleaner or an insurance policy, you can compare the products on the market and the terms of sale. You can choose the product or service which gives you the **best value for money.**

 What other services are provided by consumer organizations?

Most consumer organizations have **a threefold remit:**

- informing consumers;

- protecting consumer interests;

- lobbying for consumer-friendly policies.

Apart from information, the organizations can provide consumers with practical help in the event of problems;

hence, certain organizations provide **legal advice**. Most organizations have the right to sue in order to protect collective interests.

Some long-standing associations offer an even wider range of services, though as a rule you have to pay for them: hints for home builders, advice on gardening, DIY and energy consumption, software for calculating mortgage costs or your precise tax bill, advice for job seekers, assistance in consolidating your finances should you get heavily into debt, etc.

 So information is available on purchases I make at home. But what if — as you suggested — I want to make the most of the single market and shop abroad?

In a larger market it is of course more difficult to get hold of reliable information. But **don't be put off!** The abolition of borders between the Member States of the European Union is a **real opportunity** for the informed consumer.

National consumer organizations are beginning to look beyond the borders, because they see that the interest is there. In many cases, they can already guide you to bargains and tell you what pitfalls to avoid. Likewise, tests and surveys have increasingly assumed a 'European' dimension through cooperation and pooling of resources, **encouraged and subsidized by the European Commission.** One advantage of this procedure is that the organizations involved can save money and cross-border comparisons have become easier.

Moreover, you can also consult one of the **cross-border consumer information centres.** These centres already exist in 10 cross-border regions (see map below). They were created to provide consumers with specialized information and advice on questions or problems with a **cross-border dimension.** Examples of cases dealt with:

- Can a German manage his finances via an account in the Netherlands?

- What red tape is involved in importing a car from Spain to France?

- What remedies does a Luxembourg consumer have against a Belgian dealer who has delivered damaged furniture?

Map of the cross-border information centres

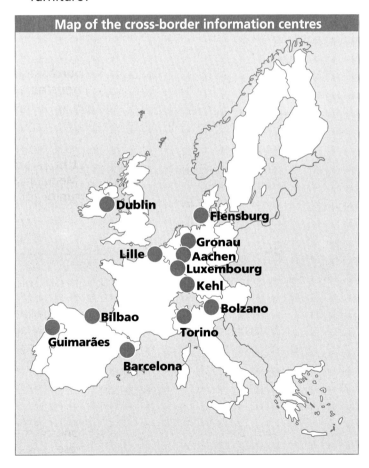

The names and addresses of the cross-border consumer information centres are reproduced at the end of this chapter.

Cross-border shopping is always complicated, if only because of language problems, not to mention foreign practices and laws. If I have a problem, what remedies are available to me?

As regards language problems, in principle it is up to you. But in border regions business people are normally used to dealing with clients from neighbouring countries and **in many cases the seller will speak your language.**

If language is a real barrier and enough is at stake — for example if you want to buy a car — there are **specialized middlemen,** who will even save you the trouble of travelling. However, beware of rogue firms and get information in advance.

As regards **trade law and practices,** it is true that substantial differences still persist from one country to another. The attendant insecurity puts off many potential buyers. Yet again, consumer protection is not uniform throughout the European Union and in all domains. However, **the differences are diminishing,** and — thanks to the work done by the European institutions in such domains as regulation of advertising, credit, sales away from business premises and contractual terms — consumers have increasing reason to feel assured that their rights and interests will be protected everywhere, irrespective of the country of purchase, the nationality of the seller, or the origin of the product.

In a nutshell, the European consumer, when he orders or buys something in another country of the European Union, will steer clear of the pitfalls he has learnt to avoid at home — and so he will not sign a contract without reading it first, not pay excessively high deposits, etc.

If — as may happen — you do run up against a problem, your best course is to **contact the closest cross-border centre** or a consumer organization, to get advice on how best to proceed. In certain cases, they may intervene on the consumer's behalf — for example, they may write to the dealer or contact the competent authorities in the neighbouring country.

✔ *But if I have to go to court?*

Only in rare cases is it in the consumer's interests to bring proceedings, for example against a dishonest seller: not only is the outcome uncertain and the procedure a costly one, but a great deal of patience is also needed.

Things become all the more complicated in the case of a cross-border dispute. While European legislation endows you with certain rights applicable in all the Member States, **the legal systems themselves remain different**. Some people see this as one of the main obstacles to the full realization of the single market. This is also the view of the European Commission, which is looking into the problem.

However, all is not lost. Many consumer disputes concern relatively small sums. A number of countries have established **simplified procedures** for disputes of this kind and in such cases it is not even necessary to be represented by a lawyer. Moreover, these procedures include simplified arrangements for bringing an action and an initial attempt at conciliation (mandatory in most cases) by the court dealing with the case.

Simplified procedures in the Member States of the European Union

Member State	Procedure	Ceiling
Belgium	Juge de Paix / Vrederechter (Justice of the Peace)	BFR 75 000
Denmark	Forbrugerklagenævnet (Central Commission for Consumer Complaints) and Ankenævn (sectoral commissions)	No ceiling
Germany	Amtsgericht (local court)	DM 10 000
Greece	Ειρηνοδικείο / Irinodikio (Justice of the Peace)	DR 150 000
Spain	Juicio verbal (oral hearing)	PTA 80 000
France	Saisine simplifiée (simplified procedure)	FF 13 000
Ireland	Small claims procedure	IRL 5 000

Italy	Giudice di Pace (Justice of the Peace)	LIT 5 000 000
Luxembourg	Juge de Paix (Justice of the Peace)	LFR 200 000
Netherlands	Kantongerecht (cantonal court)	HFL 5 000
Austria	Bezirksgericht (district court)	ÖS 100 000
Portugal	Processo sumarissimo (rapid procedure)	ESC 250 000
Finland	Kuluttajavalituslautakunta / Konsumentklagonämnden (Complaints Commission)	No ceiling*
Sweden	Allmänna Reklamationsnämnden (Complaints Commission)	No ceiling*
United Kingdom (except for Scotland)	Small claims scheme	UKL 1 000
Scotland	Small claims scheme	UKL 750

* A 'ceiling' may be applied by certain Complaints Commissions depending on the economic sector to which the dispute relates.

All the Member States also have out-of-court procedures (i.e. without involving a judge) especially for disputes of this kind (e.g. arbitration) and mediators or ombudsmen responsible for different sectors (often public services such as telephone, water, general government, etc.). Moreover, recognized consumer organizations and in certain cases administrative agencies are entitled to bring proceedings to protect collective interests. The situation in the different Member States is summarized below:

■ Belgium

There are arbitration procedures in the following three sectors: laundries, furniture, and travel agencies. Representative actions may be brought by consumer associations in some specific domains. The Liège and Ghent bars have created two advice bureaux for citizens of those cities: they charge only moderate fees.

■ Denmark

The Central Commission for Consumers Complaints hears consumer disputes, the complainant paying a modest fee. Procedures take an average six months. The 'consumer ombudsman', created in 1975, has a general mandate – to protect all consumers – with the focus on preventing infringements of the law.

■ Germany

The conciliation offices of the Chambers of Commerce and Industry handle approximately 10 000 cases per year, of which 90% are settled amicably. There are also local conciliation committees in the former GDR. Moreover, there are ombudsmen in sectors such as banking services. Consumer associations also have the right to bring proceedings in certain circumstances.

■ Greece

The new Consumer Protection Act of 16 November 1994 grants consumer organizations the right to approach the government and the courts to obtain legal protection for their members' rights.

Likewise, these organizations are entitled to sue, to demand the adoption of interim measures and to be a party to cases involving their members.

Consumer associations with at least 50 active members may also bring class actions.

■ Spain

Consumer protection is enshrined in the Constitution itself. On the basis of this principle, a free arbitration system has been created specifically for consumer disputes, the objective being to regulate all disputes of a consumer nature. Consumer organizations are entitled to bring proceedings in the event of unfair competition.

■ France

There is a single address in each *département* for all information or problems relating to consumer affairs: PO Box

5000. The *Directions Départementales de la Concurrence et la Répression des Fraudes* (DDCRF) redirect incoming enquiries to the appropriate agencies and see to their follow up.

Recently a number of `Commissions for settling Consumer Disputes' were set up in certain départements on the basis of a decree issued on 20 December 1994.

Approved consumer organizations (cf. Annex A) may bring either the actions of collective interest provided for in the Act of 5 January 1988, or 'joint representation actions', whereby several consumers who have been harmed individually may 'authorize' an association to sue for damages.

A simplified procedure (déclaration au Greffe) exists for disputes of up to FF 13 000, which are heard by the district courts (Tribunaux d'instance).

■ Ireland

Several out-of-court procedures have been established at the initiative of sectors of the economy. Examples include the ombudsmen for insurance services and credit institutions. The Director of Consumer Affairs, who has been invested with certain powers, is statutorily independent. The Consumers' Association is responsible for providing information and assistance to individuals in certain cases.

■ Italy

National arbitration procedures cover telecommunications services. Moreover, each region has a *difensore civico* responsible for hearing complaints against the administration. Consumer associations may bring actions only in respect of misleading advertising.

■ Luxembourg

The Justice of the Peace has jurisdiction for disputes of up to LFR 200 000. Consumer organizations may bring proceedings to challenge unfair terms and unfair trading practices.

■ **The Netherlands**

Consumers who have unsuccessfully attempted to reach an amicable agreement with the vendor may appeal to a 'Geschillencommissie' (dispute commission). Each Commission is made up of a consumer representative, a vendors' representative, and an independent chairman. Its decision is binding on the parties. The procedure is basically a written one, but, at the request of one of the parties, a hearing may be scheduled.

Consumer organizations have a general right to institute legal proceedings.

■ **Austria**

The Bezirksgericht has jurisdiction for disputes of up to ÖS 100 000.

The Chambers of Commerce have established arbitration procedures for certain categories of disputes.

The Consumer Information Association (VKI) has the right to bring class actions to challenge unfair terms but may also support individual 'pilot cases' (and pay the costs) when instructed to do so by the Federal Ministry of Health and Consumer Protection.

■ **Portugal**

Certain public-sector organizations and some large firms have already unilaterally created arbitration systems to settle their clients' problems. Arbitration centres for consumer disputes have been established under a pilot project in Lisbon, Coimbra, Porto and Vale do Ave. Consumer associations are also entitled to bring actions to protect collective interests.

■ Finland

As in Sweden and Denmark, the consumer ombudsman plays a very important role in consumer protection, notably in bringing about the cessation of illegal practices (through negotiation and, where appropriate, by instituting proceedings).

As in Sweden, individual disputes may be referred to the Consumer Complaints Commission.

■ Sweden

The consumer ombudsman's task is to ensure that consumer protection law is complied with; to this end, the ombudsman secretariat (Konsumentverket) may directly contact the firms responsible for an illegal practice and, if negotiation proves unfruitful, may also bring a court action.

All consumer disputes may also be brought before the 'National Commission for Consumer Complaints' (Allmänna Reklamationsnämnden) and the procedure is completely free of charge.

■ United Kingdom

Pursuant to the Consumer Arbitration Agreements Act 1988, consumers may elect for arbitration as an alternative to using the courts. Most arbitrations result from procedures set out in the codes of practice drawn up by trade associations in consultation with the Office of Fair Trading. There are also arbitration procedures and ombudsmen in several sectors. The Director-General of Fair Trading is responsible for protecting consumer interests in general, and normally is entitled to bring representative actions.

Names and addresses of the European consumer information centres:

■ **Lille (F)**
Agence européenne d'information
sur la consommation
47 bis, rue Barthélémy-Delespaul
F - 59000 Lille
Tel. (33-20) 60 69 19 or (33-20) 60 60 60
Fax (33-20) 60 69 97

Outstation Mons (B)
Agence locale transfrontalière
de la consommation de Mons
Grand-Place, 22–Jardin du Mayeur
B–7000 Mons
Tel. (32-65) 84 07 38
Fax (32-65) 31 62 30

Outstation Kortrijk (B)
Euroconsument
Wijngaardstraat 48
B–8500 Kortrijk
Tel. (32-56) 23 37 03
Fax (32-56) 23 37 50

Outstation Veurne (B)
Sint Idesbaldusstraat 2
B–8630 Veurne
Tel. (32-58) 31 13 04
Fax (32-58) 31 03 77

■ **Luxembourg (L)**
Euroguichet Consommateur
Rue des Bruyères, 55
L–1274 Howald
Tel. (352) 49 60 22 or (352) 40 63 08
Fax (352) 49 49 57

■ **Torino (I)**
Agenzia Europea di Informazione
dei Consumatori
Via XX Settembre 74
I–10121 Torino
Tel. (39-11) 436 23 19
Fax (39-11) 436 23 19

■ **Barcelona (E)**
Agencia Europea de Información sobre el Consumo
Gran Via Carles III, 105/lletra 1
E–08028 Barcelona
Tel. (34-3) 33 09 812
Fax (34-3) 33 09 311

Outstation Montpellier (F)
Centre européen d'information et
d'accueil des consommateurs de
Montpellier
Rue Marceau, 18
BP 2123
F–34026 Montpellier Cedex 1
Tel. (33-67) 92 63 40
Fax (33-67) 92 64 67

■ **Gronau (D/NL)**
EUREGIO Grenzüberschreitende Verbraucherberatung
Enschederstrasse 362
D–48599 Gronau
Tel. (49-2562) 70 20 or (31-53) 61 56 15
Fax (49-2562) 16 39

■ **Aachen (D/NL/B)**
Eurokon Verbraucher-Zentrale NRW e.V.
Beratungsstelle Aachen
Bendelstrasse 37
D–52062 Aachen
Tel. (49-241) 40 45 26
Fax (49-241) 40 47 59

Outstation St-Vith (B)
Eurokon
Verbraucherschutzzentrale Ostbelgien
Beratungsstelle St.-Vith
Mühlenbachstrasse 12
B–4780 St-Vith
Tel. (32-80) 22 97 00
Fax (32-80) 22 78 80

Outstation Eupen (B)
Eurokon Verbraucherberatungsstelle
Neustraße 44
B–4700 Eupen
Tel. (32-87) 55 55 40
Fax (32-87) 55 51 33

Outstation Heerlen-Hoensbroek (NL)
Infowinkel Hoensbroek
Hoofdstraat 11
6431 LA Hoensbroek
The Netherlands
Tel. (31-45) 60 44 87
Fax (31-45) 60 44 93

■ **Flensburg (D/DK)**
Eurocon
Euro-Verbraucher/Forbruger
Information
Rathausstrasse 20
D–24937 Flensburg
Tel. (49-461) 28 705
Fax (49-461) 27 578

■ **Kehl (D/F)**
Euro-Info Consommateurs/
Euro-Info Verbraucher e.V.
Kinzigstrasse 5
D–77694 Kehl
Tel. (49-7851) 48 28 62
Fax (49-7851) 48 28 63

3. Information, advice and access to justice   **45**

■ **Guimarães (P)**
Agência Europeia de Informação
Sobre Consumo
Rua Capitão Alfredo Guimarães, 1
P–4800 Guimarães
Tel. (351-53) 51 37 00 to (351-53) 51 37 07
Fax (351-53) 51 37 09 or (351-53) 51 37 10

Outstation Pontevedra (E)
Euro-Info
Axencia Galego-Portuguesa de información
ós consumidores
Jofre de Tenorio, 1
(Pza. de C. de Arenal, Edf. Fontoira)
E–36002 Pontevedra
Tel. (34-86) 86 22 33
Fax (34-86) 86 22 41

Outstation Santiago de Compostela (E)
Axencia Galego-Portuguesa de información ós
consumidores
Avda. de A. Coruña, 6 baixo
E–15706 Santiago de Compostela
Tel. (34-81) 54 54 00
Fax (34-81) 56 21 08

■ **Bilbao (E)**
Agencia Europea de Información
al Consumidor
Calle Simón Bolívar, 27, 1°, Dpto. 12
E–48013 Bilbao
Tel. (34-4) 442 32 88 or (34-4)518 992
Fax (34-4) 427 74 02

No matter what type of information you need, the
centres listed above are there to help you. They publish
and distribute folders and brochures on various subjects
and of course they can contact the other centres in the
network.

European consumer guide to the single market

PART II

Protection of the consumer in general

4. General product safety

Shopping without fear

Free movement of goods presupposes a minimum level of product safety in all countries of the European Union. The completion of the single market should not be allowed to compromise consumer protection. Standards should be harmonized upwards rather than downwards, so that you can buy products in all Member States just as confidently as you do at home.

This is why over the years the European Union has taken measures to improve the protection of European consumers; such measures mainly concern legislation on general product safety and liability for defective products.

Results:

1. Throughout the European Union, the goods you buy have to meet a certain number of common safety standards.

2. In the event of harm sustained, you are entitled to due compensation; it is enough for you to prove the defective nature of the product and the causal link between the defect and the harm.

3 In the event of a serious and immediate hazard, emergency measures will be taken to tackle the problem.

Why has the European Union been concerned with product safety?

Firstly, one of the fundamental aims of the European Union is **to improve the living conditions of its citizens,** an objective which cannot be achieved if their safety is neglected.

Secondly, the European Community has remained very circumspect about opening the frontiers to create a large market: products circulating in the Community should be **safe products,** something which would be impossible to achieve if each country had different safety standards.

 What measures has Brussels already taken to ensure that products are safe?

Firstly, there is legislation relating to **specific products,** such as toys, cosmetic products, or pharmaceuticals (for more details on these subjects see the individual chapters of this guide) and, secondly, there are **texts with a wider scope,** namely legislation on **'liability for defective products' and 'general product safety'.**

The latter text introduces a general safety requirement designed to prevent the marketing of dangerous products: hence this legislation is of a preventive nature.

Naturally, this does not mean that all goods circulating in the large internal market are safe. But all the measures adopted in this domain should eventually achieve this objective, and they are backed up by legislation on **liability for defective products.**

 How exactly do you define 'safe products'?

In the legislation on general product safety, a safe product is **a product which, under normal or reasonably foreseeable conditions of use, does not present any risk,** or at most only the minimum risks compatible with the product's normal use.

For example, an electric drill is certainly not a safe product for a child! Thus, entrusting a child with this product cannot be considered as normal use. However, it can be considered safe when it is used by adults because they are expected to be familiar with the operating instructions, conditions of use and hazards — which must of course be acceptable.

Now for something very different: when you shampoo your hair, some of it might get into your eyes, so the formula is designed to avoid excessive eye irritation. But no one can reasonably maintain that shampoo is a dangerous product because it hurts your eyes a little. It would be dangerous, though, if you were careless enough to drink it, which is certainly not what it was made for!

 ### How can I assess safety?

The criteria for judging whether a product may be presumed safe are very clear. Firstly, the product in question must **comply with any regulations,** at national or European level, relating to the sector concerned and governing the safety of the product in question. If no specific legislation exists, conformity will be evaluated in the light of European technical specifications or, in their absence, national standards, codes of conduct and of good professional practice and, finally, the level of safety which consumers can reasonably expect.

Standards, which are crucial to the safety of electrical appliances, for example, are devised by specialized organizations which conduct research, consult experts in the domain in question, and take into account the opinion of consumers' representatives.

At European level there are three organizations, namely CEN (European Standardization Committee), Cenelec (European Committee for Electrotechnical Standardization) and ETSI (European Telecommunications Standards Institute).

Protection of the consumer in general

Does this mean that national safety rules will ultimately disappear?

Community initiatives do not automatically mean the abolition of existing national safety standards.

However, all products on sale in the European Union must satisfy a general safety requirement and national laws and standards can no longer be invoked to prohibit the marketing of products manufactured in other countries on the basis of equivalent safety levels.

 Precisely what obligations do manufacturers have to consumers?

Manufacturers may only place safe products on the market. They must inform consumers about potential risks (for example in operating instructions or usage precautions). They must also monitor their products and, in the event of problems, take the necessary measures (for example, withdrawal of a faulty product).

 And how can I check whether manufacturers are complying with their obligations? Is there an approval stamp?

 Unfortunately, the passing of legislation designed to protect your safety is no guarantee that an unsafe or even dangerous product will not appear on the European market. There is a 'CE' mark to be affixed to certain consumer goods such as household or electrical equipment, DIY tools, lawnmowers and toys (see Chapter 13). This mark, however, shows only that the manufacturer or importer claims their products comply with safety requirements and standards and it is affixed under their entire responsibility.

 Laying down standards is one thing, but who is responsible for policing their implementation?

It is up to the national authority to take the necessary measures to ensure compliance with the safety requirement. These measures include:

- sampling;

- requests for information addressed to producers or importers;

- provision of warnings on the risks associated with a product;

- ban on marketing a product or even withdrawal of a dangerous product.

Goods from non-member countries must also comply with Community rules or, in their absence, national rules. Community legislation on general product safety applies to all products intended for European consumers irrespective of the products' geographical origin.

In recent years, **a system for collecting information on accidents involving consumer products** has been established in each country. The European network for the surveillance of home and leisure accidents, known as Ehlass, helps pinpoint hidden dangers in consumer products and analyse factors which may lead to accidents.

 But suppose, despite these standards, my hair-drier begins to overheat and singes my hair. What can I do?

Well, something is wrong with your hair drier, no question about that! Hence, the manufacturer is responsible for the injury you have suffered.

But be careful! You must prove the following facts:

- that the product used is defective;

- that you have suffered harm;

- that there is a link between the two: i.e. the problem has arisen because the product was defective.

Depending on the circumstances you are entitled to claim damages for the material and/or physical harm done.

Note that you don't have to prove that the manufacturer was negligent or at fault; indeed there is only one circumstance in which the manufacturer may disclaim liability for his products, and that is if the state of scientific and technical knowledge at the time he put the product into circulation was not such as to enable the existence of the defect to be discovered.

And if the danger was really serious? Suppose my hair-drier completely burns my hair off? What kind of measures can be taken to ensure that the same thing doesn't happen again?

In such cases, it is important that the circumstances of the accident be communicated to the competent authorities at national level. **If the product in question presents a serious and immediate risk,** the national authorities of the country in which the accident has occurred will inform the European Commission via the network for the rapid exchange of information and a same-day warning will be relayed to the national authorities of all other Member States of the Union.

This system for the rapid exchange of information dates from 1984.

The national authorities are obliged to notify serious problems associated with the use of consumer products encountered on their territory, using this system. The Commission in turn notifies the other EU countries.

One recent real-life example is where the European Commission immediately notified the national authorities that a toy — a small fake grenade containing a banger — had torn off the fingers of children playing with it.

Are there special measures to protect children?

Yes! Because children are always very vulnerable, the European Union has adopted **legislation specially designed to protect them.**
Firstly, there is the Directive on **toy safety,** explained in greater detail in Chapter 13 on toys.

Secondly, since small children are likely to put anything that attracts their attention into their mouths, there is a special law which **prohibits the manufacturing and marketing of 'dangerous imitations'.** This text concerns products, which, appearing to be other than they are, endanger the health or safety of consumers. For example, they may have a form, smell, colour, appearance, packaging, labelling, volume or size, such that it is likely that consumers, especially children, will confuse them with foodstuffs. If such products are sucked or ingested they may cause suffocation, poisoning, or the perforation or obstruction of the digestive tract.

Finally, there is the **obligation** to ensure that dangerous products (such as acids or caustic liquids) have **child-proof containers** so as to protect children from the risk of swallowing liquids or other toxic products.

What should I do in the event of an accident?

Imagine your child has swallowed bleach. Clearly, you can't just wait for the authorities to do something. **You must contact the emergency services immediately**.

To simplify things, the countries of the European Union have agreed on a single number – **112** – for calling the emergency services. In due course, **and by 31 December 1996 at the latest**, this number will be installed in all 15 Member States of the Union.

In the meantime, please find on page 56a table with **the police, ambulance and fire brigade emergency numbers that currently apply** in the Member States.

Protection of the consumer in general

	Police	Ambulance	Fire brigade
Belgium	101	100	100
Denmark	112	112	112
Germany	110	110	112
Greece	100	166	
	109 (suburbs of Athens)		199
Spain	091	092	080
France	17	17	18
Ireland	999	999	999
Italy	113	113	113
Luxembourg	113	112	112
Netherlands	0611	0611	0611
Austria	133	144	122
Portugal	115	115	115
Finland	10022	112	112
Sweden	90000	90000	90000
United Kingdom	999	999	999

Some hints

Take care! Despite all efforts at Community or national level to ensure your safety, you are protected by a 'cocoon'. You must remain alert.

Raise the alarm! If you come across a product you think is unsafe, inform the competent authorities and/or consumer organizations in your country (see list of useful addresses in Annex A).

Assert your rights! Contact consumer organizations for advice as to whether you are entitled to damages. Don't forget to file all particulars concerning the manufacturer and/or supplier.

What remains to be done

Sadly, the adoption of safety legislation does not guarantee that no unsafe or dangerous products will be introduced into the European market. For example the 'CE' mark is fixed to a toy on the exclusive responsibility of the manufacturer or importer, without other monitoring bodies being involved. Rogue operators may try to penetrate the intra-Community market and hence accidents may still occur.

This is why EBCU (European Bureau of Consumers' Unions) has been calling for a European mark of conformity with common standards, readily identifiable for consumers and backed by independent tests.

5. Canvassing

Don't fall for the soft sell!

Doorstep selling and related practices have a long tradition dating back several centuries. However, in the modern world, with its plethora of choice, this practice presents a number of risks for the consumer, especially as regards:

- the possibility of comparing the quality and price of the goods or services on offer;
- familiarity with and knowledge of the conditions of sale or the contractual terms.

For this reason the European Union has endeavoured to maximize consumer protection by adopting European legislation.

The rights conferred by this legislation are simple but substantial:

- introduction of a cooling-off period;
- the right to rescind a contract within a specified time limit.

But take care! This legislation is of limited scope and certain types of contract are excluded.

Protection of the consumer in general

Somebody has knocked on my door and wants to sell me some gym equipment. Is this doorstep selling?

Yes! Let's get it straight: **canvassing or doorstep selling is where a seller approaches you without your having expressly asked him,** and you are outside business premises.

Then you are in a situation covered by **European legislation on contracts negotiated away from business premises:**

- if a seller, on his own initiative, visits you at your home or place of work;

- if, for example, you have been invited to join an excursion whose purpose is to present products to you;

- if you have been invited to join a sales party at a neighbour's house, over a cup of tea, for example.

This European legislation applies to selling techniques of this kind applied both in your own country and in a cross-border context (for example in the context of a promotional outing).

 I have ordered a set of encyclopaedias from a salesman who visited my home without an invitation. Can I, after thinking it over, turn down his offer?

Naturally! If a representative knocks on your door, you are legally protected no matter what country of the Union you reside in.

The seller must, **on signature of the contract, hand you a written information notice.** This document, which must be dated, must **inform you of your right to rescind the contract.** It must also clearly mention the name and address of the trader and supplier, as well as particulars enabling the contract to be identified.

You have the right to renounce the effects of this undertaking **by sending your notice of withdrawal before ex-**

piry of the time limit granted to you. Be careful! Don't forget to send your letter by registered mail with a request for an 'acknowledgement of receipt'.

You must be given a cooling-off period of **at least seven days** from the moment the seller hands you the notice. In some countries the cooling-off period is longer. During this period, **you are not obliged to make any payments.**

 In response to a persuasive commercial, I asked a cleaning liquids salesman to drop by. He eventually convinced me to buy a dishwasher and I signed the order form. The day after I changed my mind and told him I wanted to back out. Am I entitled to do so?

In such cases you are protected. The legislation covers situations in which a trader sells you a product other than the one corresponding to your original request, provided you were unaware at the time that this was one of the services offered by the seller.

However, **it does not provide protection** if you ordered a product after asking for a demonstration or after sending in a reply coupon requesting documentation on the product.

 If I sign an insurance policy, do I have the same rights?

Unfortunately not! **Insurance is one of the categories of contracts which are exempted from these rules.**

Neither can you rely on the legal protection under this Directive should you wish to:

■ purchase a building;

■ purchase securities;

■ rent immovable property (including timeshares).

Community legislation also excludes contracts for the supply of foodstuffs, beverages or other goods intended for current consumption supplied by regular roundsmen.

Neither are you protected by this legislation if you have signed a contract for the supply of goods or services after consulting a catalogue, in the absence of the seller. This comes under the rubric of distance selling, to which quite specific rules apply (see Chapter 6 on distance selling).

So if I want some repairs done to my flat, I have no remedy.

Transactions concerning the supply of services and their incorporation in immovable property or contracts relating to the repair of immovable property do come within the remit of this legislation. If, for example, a painter — a supplier of services — proposes to do work in your home **without your asking him,** this is doorstep selling. So you may change your mind before he starts work. However, if you yourself take the initiative and ask for a quote for home improvements, this is not doorstep selling and the Community rules do not apply.

Is doorstep selling authorized in all countries of the Union?

It has to be said that many people are unhappy with this selling technique; hence, a number of countries have adopted rules which are stricter than the legislation that applies at Community level.

For example, **Denmark** and **Luxembourg** have introduced an outright ban on doorstep selling. **French** law is in many ways more protective than European legislation and it applies, for example, to such sales techniques in connection with the hiring of documentation or teaching aids. **Belgium** has adopted a law covering commercial practices and on the information and protection offered to the consumer.

Some hints

The firm won't allow you to back out? Don't hesitate to complain! Always demand a duplicate of your contract, properly drafted. Don't pay a deposit on the strength of a visiting card or the vague promise of receiving something later on.

The seller proposes a date other than that of signature of the contract? Decline the invitation. And — this is very important — date and sign the contract in your own hand. Don't forget that some shady operators may antedate the form to circumvent the law and hence deprive you of your right to back out.

The trader proposes that you make a deposit. Before delivery and before expiry of the cooling-off period, it is very risky to start shelling out cash. Are you sure you will receive the products? Be sure not to pay the seller in cash or by cheque or by authorizing him to deduct money from your account. And beware of such ploys as getting you to post-date the cheque by eight days.

You agree to pay a deposit and are cordially invited to sign a cheque without bothering to fill in the beneficiary's name. Don't be drawn in! This will save you endless bother and the risk of learning one day that your cheque has been cashed by a firm you have never heard of!

What remains to be done

Legislation on contracts negotiated away from business premises does not cover securities, the sale of immovable property, or insurance policies. The omission of insurance is all the more regrettable in that several countries allow doorstep selling techniques for insurance policies. This is a pity because of the potentially major risks in a Community environment characterized by the freedom to provide services (see Chapter 19 on insurance).

6. Distance selling

Still a risky business

Have you ever considered shopping abroad without having to travel? Taking advantage of bargains without travelling or traipsing from one store to another?

In the past few years, thanks to the boom in such new communication techniques as teleshopping, minitel and fax machines, distance selling has been given a new lease of life.

In the nascent single market, there is a risk that unscrupulous firms will take advantage of you.

The European Union has accordingly responded to the need to protect consumers against aggressive selling techniques, such as invoicing people for goods they never ordered. Legislation to protect you against these abuses and to give you identical rights throughout the European Union in respect of contracts negotiated at a distance, has been adopted and will probably enter into force in 1998.

Protection of the consumer in general

65

If I order something by teleshopping, am I protected?

European law on 'contracts negotiated at a distance' regulates several varieties of transactions of this type, including teleshopping.

We speak of distance selling when there is no direct contact between the trader and the consumer, and where the trader is seeking custom in print or via electronic means of communication (for example a catalogue, mailshot, small ads, minitel, fax, telephone, etc.). When you order something from a distance, you cannot see exactly what you are buying. Moreover, certain radio or television spots are often too fast for you to think about it. This is why specific protection is necessary.

So what kind of protection is envisaged in European legislation on distance selling?

The most important provisions are:

- the obligation to grant a seven-day cooling-off period;

- the provision of complete information;

- protection against abuse.

Thus your first right is **that you have a cooling-off period of seven working days** to decide whether you really do want to buy the product or whether you would prefer to back out of the contract. In the case of services, this time limit begins to run from the moment you receive the documents indicating the supplier's explicit agreement. During this cooling-off period you are entitled to a refund if you are not satisfied.

When the contract involves several deliveries, the cooling-off period begins the day after the first delivery.

In the event of dispute it is up to the seller to provide proof of the conditions of sale, your consent to the contract and the fact that you solicited it.

If you made a credit agreement with the supplier, the Community legislation provides for the agreement to be cancelled if you do not proceed with the purchase.

 If I back out of the contract, can the trader demand compensation?

You are not obliged to pay compensation if you rescind the contract. Of course this does not apply when the articles have been consumed or damaged.

 What information must the seller include in his offer?

Your contract must be worded in clear and precise terms in the same language as the one used in the commercial solicitation. You must be provided with the following information in writing:

- the identity of the trader;

- the characteristics of the products;

- the price to be paid.

If the supplier's identity is not stated clearly, refuse the deal or ask for the firm's particulars, i.e. **a real address.** Don't settle for a mere post office box address.

Your contract must also state:

- how long the offer is valid;

- payment arrangements, including credit terms or terms for payment by instalments;

- time limits for supply or performance;

- the conditions under which the products may be returned or replaced (where relevant, with details on the costs of such arrangements).

If the contract provides for performance in stages (for

example, volumes of an encyclopaedia to be mailed each month over a two-year period), the manufacturer must clearly state the conditions applying to withdrawal.

All costs incumbent on you, including any associated with delivery of the articles, must be clearly included in the total price to be paid. You must also be informed of any charges for the use of certain means of communication at a distance when you transmit your order or in connection with performance of the service.

Moreover, **at the latest on delivery,** you must receive a document recapitulating all the above particulars and identifying clearly the distance-selling firm with which you are dealing.

 ### *Am I protected in the event of unsolicited goods?*

Absolutely! The supplier must respect your freedom. It is up to you to agree that he provide you with the products or services. Hence you are not obliged to pay for a parcel or to return it at your expense — if you have neither requested it, nor seen it, nor touched it, nor tried it out — on the pretext of having tacitly accepted it.

No two ways about it. All solicitations must mention their commercial objective. For example, if a package is a free sample, this must be clearly indicated.

Remember that if you do not reply nobody may interpret your silence as consent. Likewise, if you do not return a product, the sender cannot conclude that you have agreed to buy it.

If you are fed up with being inundated by commercial offers, catalogues and mailshots, just because you once took up an offer of this kind, you should know that the European Union has adopted legislation on the protection of personal data which will enter into effect in 1998; pending this, you may contact these firms not only to avoid receiving their advertising but also to instruct them not to divulge your name and address to other firms (you will then be registered on what has become known as a 'red' or 'Robinson' list in certain countries).

 Since the Community legislation is not yet in force in my country, what is the situation at present?

A **European convention on cross-border mail order and distance sales** was signed in April 1992 by the members of the European Mail Order Traders Association (EMOTA).

This convention **is in no way legally binding**: the firms have agreed to a code of conduct, although they are not obliged to comply with the principles governing this agreement.

 What is the scope of this convention?

The signatory companies have undertaken:

- to make their motto 'satisfaction or your money back';

- to inform you of the use made of data relating to you and also of your right to rectify and access your file;

- to be clearly identified by their clients;

- to mention clearly in their offers the respective commitments of seller and client;

- to communicate to you, at the latest on execution of the order, the conditions and limitations of the offer, financial particulars (price, mailing costs, credit arrangements, etc.), delivery deadlines, rules governing exchange, return, refunding, after-sales services, guarantees, etc.;

- to state that the client is entitled to a cooling-off period of at least seven working days from the date of delivery, and to reimbursement in the event of excessive delivery periods or of rejection of the order as supplied;

- to inform you, within 30 days or a time limit stipulated in advance, if it is impossible to supply the articles; the seller will propose a new time limit or the cancellation of your order, with a refund if the items have been paid for in advance;

- to comply with the laws and rules of the country in which the offer has been made.

Is there legal protection at national level?

In **Ireland** and the **Netherlands** there is no legislation governing distance selling! However, there is a general contractual provision in the Netherlands that grants you an eight-day cooling-off period.

In all other countries of the European Union, legislation on distance selling exists but the protection offered differs greatly. For example, in **Germany** and the **United Kingdom**, the cooling-off period is two weeks! But there is a bit of a snag in **Germany** in that the agreement is only a contractual one — the rules have been developed via case law on telephone canvassing.

In **Spain** only Catalonia, Aragon, Galicia and Valencia have specific rules on distance selling. Elsewhere in Spain you are simply referred back to the broad principles set out in the General Act on the Protection of Consumers and Users.

Finally, in **Italy** the same rules apply to distance selling as to doorstep selling. There is also legislation which applies to certain very specific cases.

Are time limits for delivery guaranteed when I place a mail order?

Currently there is no Community text laying down time limits for delivery in connection with mail orders and laws vary from one country to another.

In several countries, such as Germany and Belgium, the buyer is free to refuse the goods in the event of a delay, whereas in the United Kingdom this option exists only if the time limit was stipulated as an essential part of the contract. In Denmark, only a major delay in delivery gives the purchaser the right to back out of the contract. Hence, **get precise information** on the rules of the coun-try that interests you, by consulting a consumer organization.

 ### How is VAT settled in connection with distance selling?

Mail order *aficionados* should know that, when they place an order with a firm in another EU country, VAT will now be included in the price and the goods will be sent directly to them. Red tape at the customs is now a thing of the past.

As to the VAT rates applicable in such cases, distance sel-ling — at least until 31 December 1996 — is one of the forms of intra-Community transactions to which the general rules do not apply.

When you order products from another EU country, you will pay VAT either at the rate applicable in your country or at the rate applicable in the seller's country (see Chapter 2 on VAT).

 ### What should I do in the event of a dispute?

If you cannot resolve your dispute amicably, you should in principle **bring an action before the court of the country in which the supplier is established,** provided the supplier is operating directly from this country. But normally you may also file a suit with the court of your own country. However, remember that the courts do not necessarily apply the law of your country of residence in resolving the problem. In the domain of distance selling, litigation is anything but a piece of cake! (see Chapter 3 on informa-tion, advice and access to justice).

Some hints

Proof of return: file all documents relating to your order because, if you return the items, you have to produce a document proving that you have done so.

The moment you commit yourself is crucial: the contract is final once the seller receives your letter of acceptance. And remember that an agreement made by fax or telex is also binding.

And moreover – never forget only your signature commits you!

What remains to be done

The legislation does not govern advertising techniques. However, certain practices such as `sweep-stakes' open only to purchasers remain truly unfair. Moreover, in teleshopping, the speed and slickness of presentation often detract from consumer information, giving customers neither the opportunity nor even the time to grasp all the implications.

Unfortunately, the law does not regulate guarantee funds or insurance policies. It is true that people are recommended not to make deposits, but what can be done when overly trusting consumers pay up front for something they never receive? Let us not forget that certain suppliers require that the order be paid for in advance, either in full or in part.

Bespoke products, contracts governing supplies, foodstuffs, beverages and other household goods are not covered by the Community legislation. A pity!

The right of rescission does not apply to services either if an essential part of their performance is due to begin before the end of the seven-day period. Likewise excluded are transactions relating to securities or other products or services whose prices are linked to fluctuations in a financial market beyond the supplier's control.

7. Contracts

Goodbye to unfair terms

In order to make the most of the single market consumers must be sure that they are soundly protected, in all Community countries, against unfair practices. Hence the Community has taken measures to combat unfair terms in consumer contracts.

Since 1 January 1995, thanks to progressive Community legislation, consumers are no longer bound by unfair terms, without the contract's validity being affected as a result. Hence the consumer is no longer helpless in the face of suppliers who include unfair conditions in a contract.

Protection of the consumer in general

But what exactly is an unfair term?

Briefly, a term in a contract may be considered in principle to be unfair if it creates **'a significant imbalance' between the rights and obligations of the consumer and those of the seller or supplier** and has not been explicitly negotiated by the two parties.

Let's take an example to make things clearer. Imagine you hire a car for your holidays and the contract stipulates that the firm is not responsible in the event of an accident caused by a defect in the vehicle. This means that if the brakes fail and you run into the first wall you meet it is up to you to shell out. This is obviously an unfair term.

Another example is that of a contract containing a term permitting a trader to change unilaterally the terms themselves, or again an insurance contract that is automatically renewed unless the policyholder makes a notification to the contrary more than six months before the expiry date.

Fine! So if my contract contains a term like this, does that mean the term is invalid?

If your contract contains a term which you consider unfair, you have the right to challenge it, or simply to ignore it.

If the trader disagrees with you, he will have to file a suit and it will be up to the courts to decide whether the term is unfair under Community law.

And if the term is indeed unfair, does that mean that it is null and void?

An unfair term in a contract is in no way binding. However, the nullity applies only to the unfair term as such **and the other terms of the contract remain valid.**

That's all very well, but the problem with contracts is that they are often difficult or impossible to understand. So it is by no means easy to interpret a contractual term oneself.

Indeed. This is why Community legislation also stipulates that terms must be drafted in a clear and understandable way. **In the event of doubt as to the meaning of a term, only the interpretation most favourable to you will be upheld.**

If the term is unclear, ask for advice from a consumer association or from another organization that can provide you with supplementary information.

 Consumer associations on the lookout for unfair terms in standard contracts

Consumer associations have an important role to play in combating unfair terms. They are entitled to bring actions on behalf of consumers before the courts or competent administrative instances to determine whether the terms in a standard contract are unfair and, if so, to have them banned. Such actions may be brought against a number of traders or suppliers in a given economic sector or their trade associations should they use similar contractual terms.

 And do these rules apply to all contracts?

These rules have applied since 1 January 1995 to all contracts concluded between a seller or supplier and a consumer.

However, they do not apply to a contract signed in the course of your business activities or to transactions between consumers, such as, for example, the sale of second-hand goods. Nor do they apply to labour contracts or contracts pertaining to the law of inheritance, or to

Protection of the consumer in general

undertakings relating to family status and the establishment of companies.

One other exception: the rules do not cover terms which have been negotiated individually between you and the trader or supplier of services, i.e. terms drafted by common agreement between the 'seller' and the client. However, the other parts of the contract which have not been negotiated are of course subject to the rules.

Some hints

Deposits and part-payments: pay attention to the meaning of these words when you sign a contract in a language other than your own. They may even be ambiguous in certain languages! In France, any payment you may make is considered as a deposit unless the order form specifies that it is a part-payment. In Belgium, the opposite applies! If the word 'deposit' is not clearly mentioned, any payment is considered as a part-payment.

It makes a big difference!

We speak of a 'deposit' when the consumer can relinquish the sale and forfeit the sum he has paid to the seller. In some countries, however, if the trader backs out of the sale, he must pay the consumer double what he has received. The part payment represents part of the total price to be paid. In a way it enables the consumer to give substance to his commitment. If the consumer wishes to repudiate the contract, the seller may demand compensation which is greater than the sum of the part-payment.

Contract: a contract is not just a piece of paper headed 'contract'. An order form, an order letter, and an estimate are also a form of contract between a consumer and a trader.

What remains to be done

As with many laws designed to protect consumers, unfair terms cannot be eliminated without the active involvement of consumers.

Consumers must remain vigilant and, whenever they come across unfair terms in a contract, should notify them to consumer associations or even complain to the competent authorities.

It will take some years' practical experience for us to judge whether this legislation has achieved its objective.

Illustrative list of unfair terms

Since contracts are documents of great legal import – and hence contain much legalese – it is very difficult to give examples of `unfair terms' in a clear and simple language.

To give you some idea as to what constitutes an 'unfair term', here are some **extracts from the list contained in the Community legislation**. To make the list more understandable, we have shortened certain sentences and slightly modified the language used. This list should not be considered as exhaustive and definitive.

Terms are to be considered as unfair which have the objective or effect of:

(a) excluding or limiting the legal liability of the seller or supplier in the event of the death of, or personal injury to, a consumer resulting from an act or omission of that seller or supplier;

(b) inappropriately excluding or limiting the legal rights of the consumer *vis-à-vis* the seller or supplier or another party in the event of total or partial non-performance or inadequate performance by the seller or supplier of any of the contractual obligations;

(c) making an agreement binding on the consumer, whereas provision of services by the seller or supplier is subject to a condition whose realization depends on his own will;

Protection of the consumer in general

(d) permitting the seller or supplier to retain sums paid by the consumer where the latter decides not to conclude or perform the contract, without providing for the consumer to receive compensation of an equivalent amount from the seller or supplier when the latter is the party cancelling the contract;

(e) requiring any consumer who fails to fulfil his obligations to pay a disproportionately high sum in compensation;

(f) authorizing the seller or supplier to dissolve the contract on a discretionary basis where the same facility is not granted to the consumer, or permitting the seller or supplier to retain the sums paid for services not yet supplied by him where it is the seller or supplier himself who dissolves the contract;

(g) enabling the seller or supplier to terminate a contract of indeterminate duration without reasonable notice except where there are serious grounds for doing so;

(h) automatically extending a contract of fixed duration where the consumer does not indicate otherwise, when the deadline fixed for the consumer to express this desire not to extend the contract is unreasonably early;

(i) irrevocably binding the consumer to terms with which he had no real opportunity of becoming acquainted before the conclusion of the contract;

(j) enabling the seller or supplier to alter the terms of the contract unilaterally without a valid reason which is specified in the contract;

(k) enabling the seller or supplier to alter unilaterally without a valid reason any characteristics of the product or service to be provided;

(l) providing for the price of goods to be determined at the time of delivery or allowing a seller of goods or supplier of services to increase their price without in both cases giving the consumer the corresponding right to cancel the contract if the final price is too high in relation to the price agreed when the contract was concluded;

(m) giving the seller or supplier the exclusive right to determine whether the goods or services supplied are in conformity with the contract or giving him the exclusive right to interpret any term of the contract;

(n) limiting the seller or supplier's obligation to respect commitments undertaken by his agents or making his commitments subject to compliance with a particular formality;

(o) obliging the consumer to fulfil all his obligations where the seller or supplier does not perform his;

(p) giving the seller or supplier the possibility of transferring his rights and obligations under the contract, where this may serve to reduce the guarantees for the consumer, without the latter's agreement;

(q) excluding or hindering the consumer's right to take legal action or exercise any other legal remedy, particularly by requiring the consumer to take disputes exclusively to arbitration not covered by legal provisions, unduly restricting the evidence available to him or imposing on him a burden of proof which, according to the applicable law, should lie with another party to the contract.

Take care! There are limitations to points (g), (j) and (l) in the case of contracts for certain financial services.

8. Advertising

Information or propaganda?

With the opening of the borders, the variety of products coming from the 15 Member States has been growing from day to day. How can we come to terms with this profusion of attractive but often overlooked products?

Advertising claims to be able to help you choose. But if a message is unreliable you may buy the wrong things. So it is essential for you to be protected against certain questionable advertising techniques and practices.

Hence the European Community has laid down certain rules for advertising with a view to strengthening:

• your right to have your economic interests protected;

• your right to correct information;

• the obligation on the advertiser to prove the truthfulness of the claims made in his advertising messages.

Protection of the consumer in general

How can I recognize misleading advertising?

If you find a flyer in your letter box advertising cut-price TV sets and turn up at the store to find that only regular-price sets are available, you are a victim of misleading advertising.

You are a victim of misleading advertising if the advertiser makes partially or completely incorrect claims concerning:

- the characteristics of the goods or services;

- the availability of the goods or services;

- the price or quantity of the goods;

- the manner and date of manufacture or supply;

- the geographical or commercial origin of the product or service;

- the expected results or the results of tests performed on a product or service;

- the conditions applicable to the delivery of products or the supply of services;

- the identity and qualifications of the advertisers.

NB: Advertising may be considered as misleading **in regard to both the content and presentation** of its message.

 What are the sectors most affected?

Experience shows that the past masters of misleading advertising work for firms that market gadgets, substances 'beneficial to health' and miracle beauty products which promise that your fatty tissue will melt away like snow in the sun or that your hair will be restored again in a twinkling.

Take care: scams abound in distance selling with its countless lotteries, and in the job market, with promises of lucrative home-working jobs or profitable sidelines, or again in property where you may be promised a place in the sun abroad (see also Chapter 17 on housing and time-shares).

Do I have to prove that the advertising has misled me?

All you have to do is to say that you have been misled, or that you consider the data contained in an advertisement to be misleading. It is then up to the advertiser to prove that the information he has provided is correct.

You do not have to prove actual loss or that the advertiser has been negligent, or a genuine intention to mislead the consumer.

If matters come to a head, the case may go to court, and the court may impose penalties. For example, in the case of firms that do not comply with the rules concerning drugs advertising, the responsible health authorities may even withdraw the authorization to market the product.

Is television advertising subject to specific controls?

Rigorous criteria have been established to protect viewers from potentially damaging influences.

Televised programmes which can be picked up in other countries must respect certain rules: strict conditions apply to the frequency of commercials, the duration and type of programme interrupted, as well as the time of broadcasting and the advertising techniques used.

Moreover, **commercials must be identifiable as such.** They may not be presented in an indirect fashion. For example, if in a film the hero removes a packet of Marlboro from

Protection of the consumer in general

his pocket, places it visibly on the table and takes his time smoking a cigarette, this is considered an indirect form of advertising.

Likewise outlawed is **'surreptitious advertising'** in the guise of information. Advertising may only be inserted for a certain number of minutes, in such a way that the integrity and value of the programme is not prejudiced. The viewer should not be bothered by isolated advertising spots.

Likewise it is forbidden to insert commercials into:

- programmes of less than 30 minutes;

- religious programmes or programmes intended for children;

- news programmes and documentaries.

TV advertising for the following products is more strictly regulated:

- cigarettes (advertising prohibited) and other tobacco-based products;

- medicinal products;

- alcoholic beverages.

 ### TV advertising

The European Union says 'no' to commercials which:

- are offensive to human dignity;

- include any discrimination on grounds of race, sex or nationality;

- encourage behaviour prejudicial to health or to the safety of consumers or to protection of the environment;

- exploit the inexperience or credulity of minors to encourage them to buy products or services or to encourage their parents to buy the goods being advertised;

- exploit the special trust minors place in parents or other persons;

- unreasonably show minors in dangerous situations;

- offend political or religious convictions.

What are the rules concerning TV drugs commercials?

Medicinal drugs or medical treatment available on prescription may not be advertised on TV.

However, products sold over the counter may be advertised on television, radio or in the press.

NB: The reference country is the one in which the television channel is located. Moreover, Member States are always free to lay down more stringent rules and to ban radio and television advertising for all drugs.

Are there also restrictions on the advertising of alcoholic drinks?

Television advertising for alcoholic beverages may not:

- be aimed at minors or depict minors consuming alcohol;

- associate alcohol consumption with an improvement in physical performance or driving or social success;

- claim that alcohol has therapeutic qualities or that it is a stimulant, a sedative or a means of resolving personal conflicts;

■ encourage immoderate consumption of alcohol or present abstinence or moderation in a 'negative' light.

 And what about cigarette advertising?

All advertising of cigarettes or other tobacco products on television or radio is prohibited.

 # Some hints

What should you do if you come across an ad you consider offensive?

Firstly, you should consult the national advertising self-regulatory body; in most countries it provides speedy and free assistance for all sorts of complaints.

In the case of television or radio advertising, always note down the time of the commercial as well as the name of the product or firm in question.

In the case of press advertising, cut out the offending item and note down the date of publication and title of the publication.

Contact a consumer association which will tell how to seek redress should this be necessary.

 # What remains to be done

Ideally consumer associations should be entitled to file suits on behalf of the victims of advertising before the courts in the advertiser's country.

Since several countries have imposed a blanket ban on the advertising of medicines, Community legislation does not offer identical levels of protection everywhere. For example, Greece already prohibits advertising of pharmaceutical products; Denmark and Belgium have banned all advertising of this type on radio and television; France has introduced prior vetting of advertising intended for the public and has banned commercials for prescription medicines.

So why don't similar rules apply to products, items, devices and methods presented as beneficial to health? The domain of the infamous 'miracle products' is after all rife with advertisements designed to dupe naive or ill-informed consumers

Protection of the consumer in general

9. Labelling

How to know everything — or almost everything — about a product

Consumers unanimously agree that the labelling of consumer products is an indispensable aid in deciding what to buy.

A label is in a way a product's identity card.

Consumers can make the most of the single market only if they are correctly and adequately informed, before and after purchase. Hence the importance of measures to encourage clear, easily readable, complete, understandable and correct labelling.

This is why better information is one of the priority objectives of consumer protection policy in the European Union.

Now that the single market has come about, do labels provide the same information everywhere?

There is no Community system covering all aspects of consumer product labelling, because it is difficult to create a single information system as long as the characteristics of the products and consumer information needs in this area remain so varied.

Community legislation relating to labelling has several aspects:

■ relatively detailed rules on prices, including both foodstuffs and non-food products;

■ ecological labels and information on energy consumption;

■ requirements as to the information provided on certain specific products, such as:

• products containing dangerous substances;

• tobacco products;

• foodstuffs;

• pharmaceuticals;

• cosmetic products;

• toys;

• textiles.

 That's fine, but without going into detail, please let me have a quick look at this legislation. Let's start with legislation on price indication.

Indication of the selling price is mandatory for all products of current consumption: the only exceptions are specific products of value such as works of art, antiques, etc.

The price must be mentioned on the label or any other support (such as a poster or tag). It must be unequivocal, easily identifiable and easily readable.

The situation in regard to unit prices is not so clear.

Price indication is mandatory for pre-packaged products sold in variable quantities — for example, pre-packaged carrots in a supermarket — as well as for products sold in bulk, such as carrots, to be packed and weighed by the purchaser.

As regards pre-packaged products in standard quantities (for example 250 g, 1 g or 1 l) laid down at Community level (remember there are also national standard quantities), the rules are of byzantine complexity, with the result that, for example, price indication is mandatory for coffee but not for tea!

However, indication of the unit price is very useful, because it makes it easier to compare rival products sold in different quantities. The Commission therefore intends to propose it be made mandatory.

 But with the new bar code system in the supermarkets, most of the products don't have any price on them!

Use of bar codes does not always make it easier to identify the price. However, **the price must be indicated somewhere** — if you can't find it on the product itself, look on the shelf where the product is stored or for a price tag in the vicinity.

If you still can't find the price of the articles you want, complain to the manager. **If you don't receive satis-**

Protection of the consumer in general

faction inform your consumer association or the national authority.

Note that to make it easier to read the prices, certain supermarkets and large stores provide their clients with bar code scanners. However, there has to be enough of them.

I see that the European Community is planning to launch an 'ecological label': what exactly is it?

Staple consumer goods and their packaging may be a major source of pollution, and many of us today only want products that impinge on our quality of life as little as possible.

The ecological label will be awarded to products which, while belonging to the same category, harm the environment less than others. If you are concerned with the quality of life, this will allow you to choose your purchases in full knowledge of the facts.

Apart from dishwashers and washing machines, toilet paper, paper kitchen towels and soil improvers — for which ecological label dossiers have already been submitted — the ecological label scheme will eventually be extended to products such as:

- paints and varnishes;

- detergents;

- shampoos;

- electric bulbs;

- shoes;

- hairsprays;

- deodorants;

- writing paper;

- insulation materials.

This system excludes foodstuffs, beverages and pharmaceuticals.

 Talking about 'ecology', the energy consumption of household appliances is an important factor: do the labels contain this kind of information?

The intention is to gradually build up an information system – in the form of an information file and a label – covering the energy consumption and consumption of other essential resources of certain household appliances such as:

- refrigerators and freezers;

- washing machines and driers;

- dishwashers;

- ovens;

- water heaters;

- light sources;

- air conditioning appliances.

These provisions will be implemented through the adoption of a specific text for each type of appliance. The diagram on page 94 is an example of a fridge label.

 Nowadays we hear more and more about accidents caused by dangerous products such as solvents, pesticides, herbicides, etc. What warnings are to be found on the labels?

Safety comes first. Labelling of dangerous or toxic substances is governed by stricter rules than those that apply

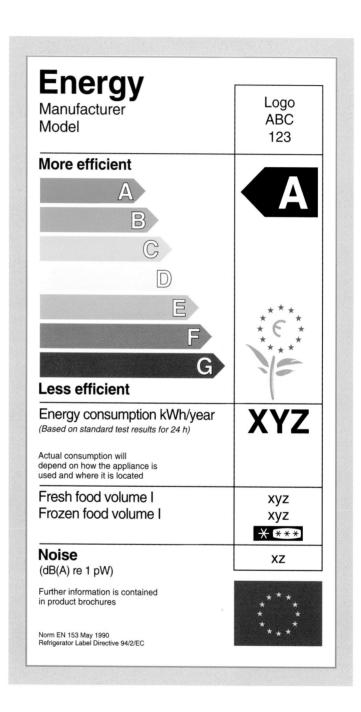

Energy

Manufacturer
Model

Logo
ABC
123

More efficient

A

B

C

D

E

F

G

Less efficient

Energy consumption kWh/year
(Based on standard test results for 24 h)

XYZ

Actual consumption will
depend on how the appliance is
used and where it is located

Fresh food volume I
Frozen food volume I

xyz
xyz

Noise
(dB(A) re 1 pW)

xz

Further information is contained
in product brochures

Norm EN 153 May 1990
Refrigerator Label Directive 94/2/EC

to normal consumer products (see Chapter 4 on product safety). All these products are labelled identically in all countries of the European Union.

Operating instructions, precautions and warnings must be provided **in the language or languages of the country of consumption or use of the product.**

There are **symbols** indicating whether a product is dangerous or toxic and which serve as warnings. They are the same in all countries of the European Union, so that consumers can immediately get the message without having to read a text. Of course this in no way means that you can ignore the labels, which may contain additional information.

As you can see on page 96, there are seven symbols, three with dual meanings: the campfire signifies 'highly flammable' and 'extremely flammable'; the skull stands for 'toxic' and 'very toxic'; the cross represents 'irritant' and 'harmful'. The other symbols signify 'explosive', 'oxidizing', 'corrosive' and 'dangerous for the environment' (See page 96).

 Talking about health hazards, does the danger of tobacco products have to be indicated?

It is generally agreed that tobacco, in its various forms, is bad for health. This thinking, as well as the desire to protect the health of young people in particular, lies behind Community legislation on the labelling of tobacco products.

Cigarette packets and packaging of other tobacco products (pipe tobacco, cigars, etc.) must bear **a warning of the associated health risks.** Each country draws up a list of the wording to be used, selected from those cited in the legislative text. Two of these are obligatory, namely:

■ 'Smoking causes cancer'.

■ 'Smoking causes heart disease'.

Protection of the consumer in general

E

ES: Explosivo
DA: Eksplosiv
DE: Explosionsgefährlich
EL: Εκρηκτικό
EN: Explosive
FR: Explosif
IT: Esplosivo
NL: Ontplofbaar
PT: Explosivo
SV: Explosiv
FI: Räjähtävä

O

ES: Comburente
DA: Brandnærende
DE: Brandfördernd
EL: Οξειδωτικό
EN: Oxidizing
FR: Comburant
IT: Comburente
NL: Oxyderend
PT: Comburente
SV: Oxiderande
FI: Hapettava

F

ES: Fácilmente inflamable
DA: Meget brandfarlig
DE: Leichtentzündlich
EL: Πολύ εύφλεκτο
EN: Highly flammable
FR: Facilement inflammable
IT: Facilmente infiammabile
NL: Licht ontvlambaar
PT: Facilmente inflamável
SV: Mycket brandfarlig
FI: Helposti syttyvä

F+

ES: Extremadamente inflamable
DA: Yderst brandfarlig
DE: Hochentzündlich
EL: Εξαιρετικά εύφλεκτο
EN: Extremely flammable
FR: Extrêmement inflammable
IT: Estremamente infiammabile
NL: Zeer licht ontvlambaar
PT: Extremamente inflamável
SV: Ytterst brandfarlig
FI: Erittäin helposti syttyvä

T

ES: Tóxico
DA: Giftig
DE: Giftig
EL: Τοξικό
EN: Toxic
FR: Toxique
IT: Tossico
NL: Giftig
PT: Tóxico
SV: Giftig
FI: Myrkyllinen

T+

ES: Muy tóxico
DA: Meget giftig
DE: Sehr giftig
EL: Πολύ τοξικό
EN: Very toxic
FR: Très toxique
IT: Molto tossico
NL: Zeer giftig
PT: Muito tóxico
SV: Mycket giftig
FI: Erittäin myrkyllinen

C

ES: Corrosivo
DA: Ætsende
DE: Ätzend
EL: Διαβρωτικό
EN: Corrosive
FR: Corrosif
IT: Corrosivo
NL: Bijtend
PT: Corrosivo
SV: Frätande
FI: Syövyttävä

X

ES: Nocivo
DA: Sundhedsskadelig
DE: Mindergiftig
EL: Επιβλαβές
EN: Harmful
FR: Nocif
IT: Nocivo
NL: Schadelijk
PT: Nocivo
SV: Hälsovådlig
FI: Haitallinen

Xi

ES: Irritante
DA: Lokalirriterende
DE: Reizend
EL: Ερεθιστικό
EN: Irritant
FR: Irritant
IT: Irritante
NL: Irriterend
PT: Irritante
SV: Retande
FI: Ärsyttävä

N

ES: Peligroso para el medio ambiente
DA: Miljøfarlig
DE: Umweltgefährlich
EL: Επικίνδυνο για το περιβάλλον
EN: Dangerous for the environment
FR: Dangereux pour l'environnement
IT: Pericoloso per l'ambiente
NL: Milieugevaarlijk
PT: Perigoso para o ambiente
SV: Miljöfarlig
FI: Ympäristölle vaarallinen

What kind of information must be mentioned on foodstuffs labels?

Rules on foodstuffs labelling are primarily designed to provide useful and objective information on pre-packaged products. The information concerns:

- the description of the product and its essential characteristics (such as price, weight, ingredients, etc.);

- perishability in the form of the best-before date or expiry date, depending on the foodstuffs and, if necessary, particular conditions regarding preservation;

- the name and address of the manufacturer and/or importer and references to the product batch.

In order to protect you against misleading information, it is forbidden:

- to provide imprecise information on the nature of the product, its consumption, quantity, the expiry date, method of production or manufacture, etc.;

- to attribute to a product effects or properties which it does not possess;

- to suggest that a product possesses particular charac-ter-istics, when in fact all similar foodstuffs possess such characteristics.

Moreover, indication of the unit price is mandatory for certain foodstuffs (for more detailed information, see Chapter 10 on foodstuffs).

And what about pharmaceuticals?

As regards information for consumers, there is first and foremost **the obligation on manufacturers to provide** an explanatory note, indicating *inter alia:*

- the drug's ingredients;

- the disease for which it is recommended and the drug's effects;

- contraindications and possible reactions;

- what to do in the event of an overdose and undesirable side-effects;

- expiry date.

The packaging itself must bear the name of the drug, the manufacturer's particulars, the expiry date and the number of the product batch. Should a problem arise, this makes it easier to trace a drug back to its origin. (More detailed information may be found in Chapter 11 on pharmaceutical products.)

 ### And what about cosmetic products?

Information on precautions to be observed in use must be mentioned on the container and packaging of cosmetic products. If these data cannot be placed on the container, an explanatory note must accompany the product. The packaging and container must also bear the words 'Best used before the end of ... ' in the case of perishable products.

From 1 January 1998 there will be an obligation to indicate the ingredients used in this type of product.

(For more detailed information see Chapter 12 on cosmetic products).

 ### ... and toys?

The obligations on the labelling on toys concern:

- affixing of the 'CE' mark testifying that the toy complies with the safety requirements indicated in the Community legislation;

- where relevant, an appropriate warning that the toy is not suitable for children under a given age;

- a possible warning on the need for adult supervision when using the toy.

(For more details, see Chapter 13 on toys).

... and textiles?

To help consumers distinguish, for example, between 'artificial silk' and genuine silk, the Community legislator has introduced requirements on labelling information concerning the fibre content of textile articles. (For more detailed information see Chapter 14 on textiles.)

Certain products are presented as being 'light', 'dietary' or 'rich in fibres': is this product information also regulated?

Claims concerning health which do not vaunt any therapeutic property — such as 'This cereal is good for your health' — are currently **regulated only at national level**. For example, such claims are authorized in the United Kingdom; hence, certain cornflake manufacturers — to come back to our example — will readily claim that 'These cereals are good for your heart'. By contrast, claims of this kind are totally banned in Belgium and Germany...and the same manufacture would be allowed to state only that the cornflakes `contain fibre'! (More detailed information may be found in Chapter 10 on food and drink.)

On the other hand, purely medical claims are out! Hence, if it is clearly stated that a product possesses curative or preventative properties — for example, a herbal tea specifically designed to help digestion and to prevent certain stomach disorders — the product in question is in fact a drug which is subject to legal rules at Community level (see Chapter 11 on pharmaceutical products).

Protection of the consumer in general

Among all these requirements on labelling, is there a rule on language use?

Community law and national laws abound with provisions on language requirements regarding consumer information, with regard to labelling, use and all other messages addressed to consumers. However, the laws are quite divergent and sometimes contradictory.

The European Union is keen to enhance the information made available to consumers in their language so that they will fully understand the labels and the directions for use. Accordingly, a new measure will soon apply this principle to foodstuffs for the first time (see Chapter 10 on food and drink).

Some hints

Read the labels! They contain lots of useful information on the product's quality.

Compare prices! Although the price of an article is rarely the only reason for buying it, the unit price (often per kilogram) can help you choose between different packagings of the same product. Even if the diversity of packagings and quantities makes price comparison more complicated, look for the unit price.

Stick up for your rights! Complain if prices are not clearly indicated.

What remains to be done

Provisions concerning labelling and other forms of information – on both products and services – are patchy and in need of improvement. Rules on price indication are not very transparent. For example, the labelling rules concerning the quantity of each ingredient in the composition of foodstuffs have not yet been approved. Again, alcoholic beverages are not covered by these provisions.

What is the exact quantity of glucides, protein, lipids, vitamins in a product? It is this kind of information that really interests consumers. Sadly, indication of the nutritional value of foodstuffs is not yet mandatory!

Nor do we yet have Community rules concerning claims of the 'light product', 'low calorie' variety. This means that in certain countries consumers are particularly at risk of falling victim to marketing claims that are sometimes misleading or even baseless.

Protection of the consumer in general

PART III

Specific sectors

10. Food and drink

On the menu: very advanced legislation

In the single market consumers can choose between food-stuffs from all over Europe. From now on, the quality of your cheese, fish or beer is no longer controlled by each national authority, but mainly by that of the country of origin.

As everybody naturally enough puts safety first, the European Union has established common hygiene and label-ling rules, to ensure healthy foodstuffs and correct informa-tion.

Consequently, staple foodstuffs are subject to strict and man-datory surveillance. The information given must be accurate. Only then will consumers have full confidence in the single market in their daily lives.

Specific sectors

I welcome the choice of foodstuffs from all over Europe. But how can I be sure that other countries are just as demanding as my own as regards their inspection arrangements?

Food accounts for a big chunk of the family budget everywhere in Europe. And seeing that it is a subject that everybody is interested in to some extent, policy makers are also concerned.

At Community level, several major legislative texts have been approved. They concern:

- labelling;

- additives;

- foodstuffs for particular nutritional uses;

- inspection and control of hygiene;

- materials in contact with foodstuffs.

Other more specific rules have also been adopted: voluntary labelling of nutritive value, standard and unique definition of the term 'organic' (although this latter measure concerns neither meat nor dairy products), etc.

 When I go shopping for groceries, what information should I find?

As regards pre-packaged foodstuffs, the label must include several items, the most important of which are:

- the name of the product;

- the list of ingredients;

- the net quantity;

- the expiry date ('use before' for perishable foodstuffs and 'best before' for other products);

- manner of use.

- Other mandatory information includes:

- the particular conditions applying to the handling or preparation of the food;

- the particulars of the manufacturer and/or seller;

- the provenance or place of origin, when the absence of such information might mislead the consumer;

- marks allowing the lot to which a foodstuff belongs to be identified.

If a product has been **irradiated** the label must say so.

The European Union institutions are currently examining the scope for improving the information given to consumers, particularly with regard to quantitative lists of ingredients and the use of languages (see Chaper 9 on labelling).

 ... and what about products that are not packaged?

Information on foodstuffs sold to consumers which have not been pre-packaged or which are packaged immediately prior to sale **are not covered by common rules at present.** It is up to the national authorities to regulate this information.

However, the Community rules clearly specify that consumers must be provided with **sufficient information.**

 Among the ingredients one often finds reference to 'additives', but generally they are only identified by numbers beginning with an E. Are there rules governing the use of additives?

The list of ingredients must include all the substances used in the manufacture or preparation of a product and which remain present in the product, including additives.

Specific sectors

Additives must be designated by their category (for example, 'colouring agent' or 'preservative'), followed by their specific 'E' number or complete name. Mention of the category of additives is required so that the consumer can **understand the purpose of the additive** in question.

The fact that an additive may have an 'E' identification number has nothing to do with its acceptability, or indeed its potential to cause harm, because this numbering system **is merely a means of identification.**

On the other hand, **an additive may only be used if it is included on the list approved by the European Union**. Inclusion on this list is authorized only after examination by the Scientific Committee on Food, whose members are experts in the fields of medicine, toxicology and nutrition.

National authorities remain free **to ban the use of an additive** – even if it is included in the Community list of authorized additives – if they consider it may imperil the health of their consumers ... though they may not prevent the free movement of the goods.

For example, ascorbic acid may not be used in France. However, this does not mean that French traders are obliged to boycott the sale of certain Italian pastries containing ascorbic acid (the substance is permitted in Italy). They may sell such pastries if they obtain a prior authorization from the French authorities.

 Claims are increasingly being made about the nutritional quality of foodstuffs: are there rules governing such claims?

Nutrition labelling is **optional:** however, if a product's packaging includes nutritional information, it must be presented in accordance with certain rules.

The information provided must belong to one of the two following groups:

- energy value, amounts of protein, carbohydrate and fat;

- energy value, amounts of protein, carbohydrate, sugars, fat, saturates, fibre and sodium.

Labels may also mention amounts of starch, polyols, mono-unsaturates, polyunsaturates, cholesterol, vitamins and certain minerals.

However, **the Community rules do not apply to certain natural mineral waters and other waters or to food supplements.**

 We have all heard about the fashion for 'light' products ... Are such claims regulated?

No. At the present time, the Commission's intention is to examine this topic as part of its existing policy on 'misleading advertising' (see Chapter 8).

 Is it important to know the geographical origin of certain products, say, champagne? Genuine champagne often costs several times as much as sparkling wine from another region in France or even from another country.

So that consumers can have correct and reliable information on the **geographical origin** of foodstuffs, labelling requirements relating to this type of information should be subject to standard rules in all countries.

Hence the European Commission is currently working on **a list of protected designations of origin and protected geographical indications,** which may only be used to label foodstuffs originating in the geographical zones concerned.

Specific sectors

These lists do not include designations of products which are already common currency and which consumers no longer associate with a particular geographical zone — even if this may have been the case originally. For example, Brussels sprouts do not necessarily have to come from Brussels!

As an extension of the thinking which led to drawing up the PDO and PGI lists, in other words being able to give certain products a higher profile, it is also possible to pro-duce a register of special products clearly distinguishable from others of the same category because of their traditional nature — either in terms of the raw materials used or by the way they are produced. Such products can be distinguished by the use of a label bearing the words 'guaranteed traditional speciality'.

 In recent years there has been a considerable increase in the demand for agricultural foodstuffs produced in a natural or 'organic' manner. Is it possible to rely on such claims?

From 1 January 1993, with a view to protecting consumers against unsubstantiated claims, foodstuffs can only be designated as 'organic' if their mode of production complies with Community rules governing organic farming, underpinned by inspections carried out by the national authorities.

The indication **'product of organic farming'** means:

■ that no synthetic chemical compound has been used in manufacturing the product;

■ that the use of chemical fertilizers and pesticides has been strictly limited.

These foodstuffs can be recognized by special labels which comply with the European code. In addition to stating organic production the label may mention that the product is subject to Community inspection arrangements, provided this product has been **packaged and transported to the retail point of sale in sealed packaging.**

Products imported from non-member countries may also make reference to organic production, but only if production complies with Community rules; it is also subject to inspection.

 It's good to get information on what one is eating, but are there any rules concerning foodstuff preparation and foodstuff hygiene?

The standard of hygiene of foodstuffs circulating freely in the single market has been improved following rules adopted in June 1993.

Generally speaking, these rules concern **foodstuffs hygiene in:**

■ all firms in the foodstuffs sector, irrespective of the type of processing;

■ mass caterers (canteens, restaurants, etc.);

■ the hospital sector.

General hygiene rules must be respected at all stages of processing, whether it be the production of goat cheese in France, the transport of Greek olives by lorry to Germany or the preservation of Danish butter in Italian shops.

However, **this text does not cover certain primary production operations** such as harvesting, or activities which are covered by specific rules (such as hygiene in slaughterhouses).

Specific sectors

Finally, inspections are performed by the **competent authorities at national level** and must be proportional to the risks. To prevent consumers being harmed by foodstuffs which are not fit for consumption or which are dangerous to human health, these inspections may lead to the foodstuffs concerned being withdrawn from the market or the firm being closed.

Does that mean that problems such as listeria in cheese or raw milk will be a thing of the past?

Products of raw milk can circulate freely in the single market. However, since January 1994 the European Community has imposed microbiological quality stand-ards on products manufactured on the basis of raw milk from cows, sheep and goats. Producers of industrial cheeses are already covered by these rules.

If meat crosses national borders, will veal treated with hormones circulate freely?

Beef, pork and mutton, as well as other products such as oils, cereals, etc. are no longer **checked** at the internal borders, but **at the place of production;** this applies to all stages in the manufacture of the product.

However the European Union has established hygiene standards and a monitoring system at the place of production, at all stages of meat processing. **It is up to the national authorities to see that these rules are complied with.**

A computerized network known as ANIMO has been established to ensure that information on the transport of live animals within the European Union is available to the national authorities. Livestock **coming from non-member** countries are subject to the same checks.

Foodstuffs of vegetable origin coming from non-member countries are subject to mandatory checks at the Community's external borders. They must meet the Community's hygiene and quality standards, and in particular are checked for possible contamination by pesticides or other dangerous substances.

Who is liable in the event of a problem?

NB: Liability depends on the circumstances. Producer liability rules do not apply to agricultural products. For example, if you get ill after eating eggs the farmer who reared the hens is not responsible because the eggs are considered as raw materials and so are not covered by legislation on liability for defective products.

However, if you are dining out and a dish prepared on the basis of eggs makes you ill, the responsibility lies with the caterer or restaurant owner.

Some hints

Read the labels and ensure that your food does not contain too many ingredients that you would rather avoid — especially if you have young children.

Don't expect consuming 'light' products to work miracles on your figure — it is more likely to lighten your wallet. This is because products of this kind are a lot more expensive than equivalent normal foodstuffs and because prices vary considerably from one brand to another.

Specific sectors

What remains to be done

Several important measures are currently on hold. This applies both to the creation of a list of additives permitted in all countries of the European Union and to the adoption of important new texts on sweeteners and colouring agents used in foodstuffs. Hence European consumers will have to wait quite some time before these rules are implemented in all the countries. If adopted as they stand, these measures would generalize the use of additives in the European Community. Certain countries would be obliged to authorize the use of additives which are currently prohibited in the preparation of some of their products.

One small problem: the draft text on additives provides that the substances must be tested individually. Hence there is no guarantee that the cumulative effects of additives made up of several substances used in the composition of one single product will not be harmful to health.

Legislation on the labelling of foodstuffs is incomplete. Additional Community rules are indispensable if consumers are to make their choices in full awareness of the facts.

11. Pharmaceutical products

One day, thalidomide set the ball rolling

Most of us recall the tragedy caused by a sedative known as thalidomide (also marketed under the name 'Softenon'). First sold in 1949 this drug, when taken by pregnant women, caused deformities in newborn children. The drug was banned, but it was already too late.

In response to this serious problem, the European Community implemented a thorough legislative programme subjecting pharmaceuticals to strict regulations. All drugs manufactured or sold in the Community now have to comply with high standards in terms of safety and effectiveness.

The measures mainly concern authorization prior to placing on the market and drug labelling and advertising. Moreover, Community legislation has created a system for the rapid exchange of information on pharmaceutical products.

Where drugs are concerned: safety comes first

What measures have been taken at Community level to guarantee consumers greater safety in regard to medicinal products?

All drugs must be monitored, registered and authorized by the national authorities **before being placed on the market.** Drug evaluation criteria are an integral part of Community law and concern the quality, safety and effectiveness of the products. Likewise, quality and safety controls are provided for during the manufacturing process.

If these tests are fully satisfactory the product may be sold throughout the Community.

On 1 January 1995, the **European Agency for the Evaluation of Medicinal Products** became operational. Its primary task is to ensure compliance with the **centralized** Community registration procedure based at the Agency. This procedure results in the issuing of a single Community authorization valid in all Member States of the Union. It is, however, applicable only to new forms of medication (such as those based on biotechnology).

Moreover, in order to be sure that drugs are properly stocked, transported and handled, the wholesale distribution of medicaments for human use is subject to supervision.

The national authorities are also authorized to apply **even more draconian inspection procedures** in the case of:

■ narcotic substances;

■ sedatives;

■ preparations based on blood plasma;

■ vaccines;

■ radioactive pharmaceutical products.

Over and above all these preventive checks, there is also a **system for the rapid exchange of information** between the national authorities and the Commission, so that pharmaceuticals with unexpected side effects can be rapidly withdrawn from the market.

 Are there specific requirements relating to the packaging of drugs to prevent children from getting at them?

Community legislation provides that all drugs placed on the market must have been approved by the national authorities; this approval must take into account not only the drug itself but also its packaging.

A warning emphasizing the need to keep the product out of reach of children must be included on the packaging, but there is no general requirement that the packaging be made child-proof as for other dangerous products (see Chapter 4 on general product safety). Each case is examined individually.

 Before taking medicine, how can I learn about possible side effects?

All pharmaceuticals intended for Community consumers **must be accompanied by a legible and detailed information leaflet.**

The information on the package or on the leaflet accompanying the drug must be complete, sufficiently visible and perfectly understandable to consumers. This applies both to over-the-counter and prescription drugs.

This information must contain particulars on the product's properties, recommended doses and possible side effects.

 But what about all those advertising campaigns?

The Community strictly regulates advertising in this domain because, even in the best of cases, it can create unwarranted expectations as to a drug's positive effects.

Specific sectors

In the worst-case scenario, advertising may also be responsible for disasters when uninformed consumers, tempted by the advertiser's blandishments, use the drug in an inappropriate manner.

Only professionals with medical training can determine in what context and in what dose a remedy may be administered. Hence it is better to avoid advertising of prescription drugs.

Advertising for drugs sold on prescription is prohibited in all media intended for the general public, being authorized only in publications intended exclusively for practitioners with medical and professional training.

Community legislation authorizes radio and television advertising of over-the-counter drugs. However, countries with a principled approach may insist on a general ban on television or radio drug commercials.

 May I purchase drugs abroad in order to benefit from lower prices?

The German authorities have long maintained that the prescription and purchase of drugs outside Germany prevents consumers from using these products in a proper manner.

However, thanks to Community legislation, pharmacists in all EC countries provide equivalent guarantees. Indeed, conditions for access to the profession of pharmacist and the way it is exercised have been harmonized. So today you can in principle freely import drugs intended for your personal use into Germany or into any other country of the European Union.

 Can I find the same drugs in another country?

Preparations with identical therapeutic effects are often sold under different names and different forms, depending on the country. For example, a drug sold as a tablet in one country may be sold as a suppository in another.

Hence, if you want to be sure of finding the same product, take along the package or the leaflet so that you can show the formula to the pharmacist in the country of purchase.

To my surprise the pharmacist sold me tranquillizers without a prescription! Yet some time ago I was not able to buy them in Italy because they were available only on prescription.

Yes it is true that there is no uniformity throughout the Member States in what constitutes a prescription medicine. Medication requiring a prescription in one country may have no such restriction in another.

Can drugs be purchased only in a pharmacy?

Any product which is expressly described or recommended for its curative or preventive properties must be considered as a drug, whether sold in a pharmacy or elsewhere. If the manufacturer or distributor addresses a brochure to the consumer praising the product's curative properties, this means that he has the clear intention of selling it as a medicinal product.

However, even if a product is not considered as a remedy under Community legislation, a Member State may subject it to the rules governing medicinal products.

Does that mean that vitamins and infusions are considered as drugs?

If it is clearly stated that the infusions or vitamins in question have curative or preventive properties, they are indeed drugs, subject to the legal rules, particularly as regards authorization for placing on the market. However, if no therapeutic properties are claimed, they may be considered as a normal foodstuff.

What about homoeopathic remedies?

This 'alternative' medicine is growing in popularity and is particularly appreciated by consumers who do not

Specific sectors

respond to mainstream remedies. To ensure that all homoeopathic drugs have a high quality level, specific legislation has been adopted.

This text simplifies the process for registering homoeopathic drugs which are marketed without any particular therapeutic indication and in very low concentrations. Other homoeopathic products remain subject to the normal notification rules.

Some hints

Never use products intended for the treatment of heart disorders without medical supervision.

Be careful with sedatives! There is a big risk of abuse. Make sure you always keep to the prescribed doses.

Be careful with new drugs which up to now have not been very widely used! Their undesirable and secondary effects may require further investigation.

Don't overdo it! It's the dose that counts. Do you know that you risk poisoning if you ingest more than seven grams of aspirin a day? This means that any drug can imperil your health if you use it wrongly. Hence the importance of heeding your doctor's advice and/or the instructions contained on the notice. Never forget to take along your prescription and the package and/or the leaflet for your drugs when you travel.

Be careful when you consult more than one doctor! Explain to each of them what has been prescribed to you by the others. Never forget that the cumulative effect of certain drugs can damage your health.

What remains to be done

Major inter-country price differentials still persist. A Europe of medicaments will only come about when price policy becomes consistent throughout the Community.

You should also remember that

drugs — such as tranquillizers — available on prescription in certain Member States may be bought over the counter in other Community countries.

In the long run, such a situation can give rise to difficulties. On the one hand, common rules concerning advertising already exist and, on the other, provisions concerning a uniform procedure for the registration of new pharmaceuticals have just been adopted ... This means there is an urgent need to harmonize the conditions under which medicines are obtained.

Specific sectors

12. Cosmetic products

Surveillance and information to encourage safe products

Cosmetic products are strictly regulated in the European Community with a view to offering you good information and optimum safety.

The Community rules focus on the composition of the products and product labelling: the ingredients of your favourite creams, sprays and deodorants should not imperil your health. And indeed the term 'cosmetic products' covers not only make-up but also a range of bodycare products such as soap, toothpaste, shampoos, etc.

Why is the European Community concerned with cosmetic products?

It's mainly a question of health and safety.

Because they are part of your daily life and because you apply them to your body regularly, cosmetic products affect your health and well-being. Hence it is necessary to ensure that the ingredients used are in no way harmful.

Fortunately, Community legislation subjects cosmetic products to **very strict controls,** particularly as regards the substances used (colouring agents, preservatives, etc.) and a list has been prepared of approximately **400 substances banned** in the composition of these products. For example, certain UV filters are authorized only under certain conditions, whereas others are prohibited.

With effect from 1997, in order to make these precautions more effective and to allow checks to be made by national authorities, the manufacturer or importer will be obliged to keep available a complete dossier on cosmetic products and their effectiveness.

 But what is meant by a 'cosmetic product'?

The legislation covers not only make-up but also many bodycare products such as soap, toothpaste, shampoo, etc.

 I'd like to know what I'm using; do the ingredients contained in cosmetic products have to be indicated?

Community legislation provides that **from 1997,** ingredients used in the composition of cosmetic products have to be indicated.

But **already,** all cosmetic products sold in the countries of the European Union must, on their container or packaging, give information concerning **precautions to be observed in use.** If these data cannot be placed on the container, an explanatory leaflet must be enclosed.

The labelling and container must also indicate 'Best used before the end of ...' in the case of perishable products.

Moreover the national authorities may require that certain information contained on the packaging be **translated into the national or official language** of the country of sale so that the consumer can understand it.

What about so-called 'natural' or 'ecological' products?

Take care! Some distinctions must be made. It is true that certain cosmetic products claim to be 'natural' and/or indicate that they have been manufactured on the basis of plants. **But these products are not governed by any specific legislation.** Likewise, the term 'ecological prod-ucts' is mere trader's hype in the absence of an ecological label. **So it is up to you to judge!**

Other products, such as sprays, may have environmentally friendly packaging in so far as it does not damage, say, the ozone layer. But let's not be naïve! Such claims do not always correspond to data validated by the competent national authorities. Often they are merely commercial gimmicks or advertising ploys.

What about products that have not been tested on animals?

The claim 'not tested on animals' is sometimes tantamount to misleading advertising. Although the final product may not have been tested on animals, it is practically certain that some of its ingredients have.

But let's be patient! Thanks to Community legislation, tests on animals are to be cut back or even eliminated as of 1998.

Specific sectors

Who shall I turn to if I have a problem — for example if my moisturizer has irritated my skin?

Despite the controls and tests carried out in manufacturing a product, the product may affect persons subject to allergies or particular reactions — irritation of the skin or eyes for example — or it may be used in an unsuitable manner by a child.

At any rate, if in doubt **the national authorities may provisionally ban the sale of a cosmetic product** which they consider dangerous to consumer health.

If you have a problem with a cosmetic product, do not hesitate to inform — preferably in writing — your shop or the manufacturer, as well as the authority responsible for safety monitoring in your country (see the 'Useful addresses annex'). It may also be worthwhile sending a copy of your correspondence to a consumer organization.

Some hints

Keep your eyes open! Labelling, display and advertising of cosmetic products often claim properties which the products do not possess. Claims may concern therapeutic properties or scientific arguments for similar products sold in pharmacies, erroneous claims as to the results to be expected, etc.

Beware of miracle products consisting of substances which 'simply banish those pimples' and creams which 'make wrinkles vanish overnight' or appliances which 'work miracles on one's figure, face or tissue'.

Beware of the soft sell in regard to this category of products, which may influence you subliminally — always read what is stated on the package and usage leaflet.

What remains to be done

Community legislation on cosmetic products is quite complete. However, in order to take into account technical progress, and because manufacturers are always introducing new ingredients, constant vigilance is required.

Moreover, combinations of ingredients may have unexpected effects, and Community legislation should take this into account.

Specific sectors

13. Toys

Your children's health and safety first and foremost!

Children — who are starting to learn about life — are the most vulnerable category of consumers and deserve our particular attention.

By definition, toys are children's prerogative. Hence the European Union has devoted particular attention to ensuring that toys are 'safe products' in all Community countries.

Specific legislation defines the physical, mechanical, chemical and inflammability requirements of all toys marketed in the European Union. It also sets out the minimum information which must be provided to the consumer. A toy's conformity with the safety requirements must be indicated using the 'CE' label.

Remember that a 'Europe of toys' cannot be a success without your help.

How can I be sure that a toy is 'a safe product' for my child?

Since 1 January 1990 all toys placed on the market or even given away within the Community must comply with the safety requirements defined by Community legislation.

 A toy's conformity with these requirements is indicated by the CE mark, which **must** be affixed by the manufacturer or his representative. The CE mark is equivalent to a **presumption** that the toy has been manufactured in compliance with well-defined standards to minimize physical, mechanical, chemical, electrical and health risks.

The two letters CE must be affixed either to the toy or on the packaging in a visible and indelible form. They may also be contained on the label or usage instructions, in the case of small toys and toys consisting of small parts.

 If the manufacturer himself affixes this mark, how can one be sure that he is not cheating?

The Member States are required to carry out sample checks on toys on sale in their country, and to ban or restrict the sale of any toy which does not comply with the essential safety requirements (even if it bears the CE mark).

Since this label is affixed by the manufacturers (or their approved representatives) and conformity is only partially controlled, it is always possible that certain unscrupulous firms may ignore the rules.

So beware! The CE mark as such is not a safety guarantee.

If, despite official policing, you are unfortunate enough to come across a toy which seems to you to be dangerous, you should inform the competent authorities in your country. They will decide as to the appropriate measures and may order the toy's withdrawal from the market.

If the toy represents a serious and immediate danger, there is a system for the rapid exchange of information by which the Commission is informed, so that it can alert the responsible authorities in all the other countries of the Union.

Are toys bearing the CE mark of better quality than the others?

Currently, all toys in the single market — whether manufactured within the Community or imported from non-member countries — must bear the CE mark.

However, the CE mark only applies to safety aspects in connection with 'normal' use and hence is not an indication of quality.

Does this legislation cover all sorts of toys? What about fireworks?

Fireworks are not covered because they are not considered as toys. The reason is very simple: these products are not intended for children, and hence they are not governed by this legislation.

Apart from fireworks, toy safety legislation excludes from its scope 20 other sorts of products, simply because they cannot be considered as toys; these products are indicated in the following list:

- Detailed scale models for adult collectors

- Slings and catapults

- Christmas decorations

- Sets of darts with metallic points

- Equipment intended to be used collectively in playgrounds

Specific sectors

- Electric ovens, irons or other functional products operated at a nominal voltage exceeding 24 volts

- Sports equipment

- Products containing heating elements intended for use under the supervision of an adult in a teaching context

- Aquatic equipment intended to be used in deep water

- Vehicles with combustion engines

- Folk dolls and decorative dolls and other similar articles for adult collectors

- Toy steam engines

- 'Professional' toys installed in public places (shopping centres, stations, etc.)

- Bicycles designed for sport or for travel on the public highway

- Puzzles with more than 500 pieces or without picture

- Video toys operated at a nominal voltage exceeding 24 volts

- Air guns and air pistols

- Babies dummies

- Fireworks, including percussion caps

- Faithful reproductions of real firearms

- Fashion jewellery for children

But even outside this list there are many toys — such as plastic scale models or chemistry sets — which can be dangerous for very small children!

Perfectly right! This is why **the legislation requires a minimum of information to guide the purchaser** in his choice.

In order to maximize safety for children, the manufacturer — or distributor — must indicate on the packaging or on the instructions for use any information capable of reducing a foreseeable risk and, notably, he must evaluate certain risks and stipulate a minimum age, such as a warning of the type 'Not suitable for children under three years'.

Other toys, which reproduce on a small scale appliances often used by adults, also present a risk. In such cases the following wording must appear on the toy or its packaging: 'Warning: to be used under the direct supervision of an adult'.

The component parts of toys such as slides, suspended swings and trapezes, must be assembled by an adult.

As regards risks associated with handling dangerous substances, particulars on the precautions to be taken and first aid to be provided in the event of accidents must be supplied. The packaging must bear the following marking: 'Warning: For children over ... years of age only. For use under adult supervision'.

 ## Some hints

Warning! Warning! Safety is everybody's concern. We urge you to read the following advice closely.

Before purchase:
Check whether there is a minimum age on the toy's packaging, to ensure that your child is not too young to use it;

check whether certain particulars are mentioned, so that you can, if necessary, identify the toy's origin: name and address of the manufacturer, his authorized representative, or the importer;

does the toy bear the CE mark?

Before use:

Check the state of the toy: if you have any doubts as to its reliability, put it back in its packaging and return it to the dealer;

look for the manufacturer's recommendations, such as 'To be used under adult supervision';

read the instructions for use and details of the toy's composition;

before throwing away the packaging, retrieve the information concerning the manufacturer — it may be useful in the event of a complaint;

if necessary, briefly demonstrate to your child how the toy works. Draw his attention to possible risks, explaining the kind of things he must avoid doing.

After use:

Check the state of the toy. If it presents a risk, after use, put it somewhere out of the child's reach. If it is damaged, have it repaired or throw it out;

never allow a toy that has become dangerous to fall into the hands of an unsuspecting person or to come within his reach;

do not hesitate to notify the competent ministry of any product which presents a risk due to a defect in manufacture or following use.

Don't forget: unless you keep your eyes open the Community legislative texts and the manufacturers' endeavours will lose much of their impact because your child is never completely safe from danger. So spare a little time to:

• explain to the child how to use the toy properly;

• supervise the child's play;

• ensure that the child uses the recommended protective accessories.

What remains to be done

Warning! The CE mark is just a presumption that the toy complies with the safety requirements of European legislation. The manufacturers themselves (or their representatives) affix the CE label to their toys without any safety test having to be performed by an independent body. The conformity policing system may have to be strengthened.

Under current rules, if a toy presents a danger, consumers do not have to be alerted directly; the European Commission informs the national authorities, who normally pass the information on to their nationals. This three-tier system is not necessarily the most effective one. Hence the mechanism should be improved in order to give it more bite.

Specific sectors

14. Textiles

Reliable information labelling

A multitude of products are on sale in the single market and consumers need useful and reliable information in order to make sensible choices. This applies in particular to clothes and other textile products.

Thus the European Union has established a **uniform system for labelling the fibre composition of textiles** available in the internal market, irrespective of their place of origin.

When I buy clothes I much prefer natural fibres, such as cotton, linen and wool. How can I be sure to make the right choice in other countries of the Union?

Information on the composition of textile fibres must accompany all clothing placed on the market in the countries of the European Union.

Community legislation lays down certain requirements concerning:

■ the names to be used for fibres that form part of a garment;

■ particulars to be included on labels;

■ other forms of marking.

These obligations, which are identical in all countries of the European Union, apply both to textiles manufactured in the Community and to imports.

 But where can I find this information?

Normally, particulars on the fibres used are to be found on the **label** affixed to the garment or other textile article.

The general rule is that, for each article, separate pieces of textile must have a **separate label.** However, when two or more products with the same fibre content constitute an ensemble — for example a three-piece suit — they only need one label.

Cloth sold by the metre or in cut lengths must be offered for sale in such a way that the customer can acquaint himself with the particulars affixed to the packaging or to the roll.

But what particulars have to be mentioned if a garment consists of several different fibres?

In this case the obligatory indications vary with the proportions of fibres in the article.

First, in the case of textile products composed of two or more fibres, one of which accounts for **at least 85%** of the total weight, three types of presentation are permissible:

■ the name of the fibre, followed by its percentage by weight;

■ the name of the fibre followed by the words '85% minimum' or

■ the full percentage composition of the product.

If however a textile product is composed of two or more fibres, **none of which accounts for at least 85% of the total weight,** the label must indicate at least the percentage of the two main fibres, followed by the names of the other constituent fibres, with or without an indication of their percentage.

For fibres which separately account for less than 10% of the total weight of a product, it is not necessary to indicate each fibre, and the words 'other fibres', followed by the total percentage, is permissible.

In the case of fibres whose composition cannot be easily be determined at the time of manufacture, the terms 'textile residues' or 'unspecified composition' may be used.

NB: All these percentages refer to the total weight, exclusive of such accessories as buttons, elastic, etc.

Specific sectors

What if the manufacturer provides inflated figures as to fibre composition?

This is plain fraud! Quantitative information must be reliable and **it is up to the authorities of each country to conduct the necessary checks.**

The Community texts have been drafted in such a way as to minimize such abuses. For example, no textile product may be qualified as '100%...' or 'pure', unless of course it is composed of one single fibre only.

Likewise, a woollen product may not bear the words 'pure wool' or 'shornwool', if it has been subjected to any spinning or felting processes other than those required for its manufacture. The texts must also be reliable as to textile particulars and names.

If however you find, say, a garment whose label you consider fraudulent do not hesitate to contact a supervisory body and/or a consumer association. **Your vigilance will help to eliminate such abuses.**

 Does this legislation also apply to textile products other than clothing and cloth sold by the cut?

Apart from the two types of product mentioned above, the legislation requires that information as to textile fibre content must be provided for:

- products containing at least 80% by weight of textile fibres;

- furniture, umbrella and sunshade coverings containing at least 80% by weight of textile components.

 But what use is this information if it is not sufficiently legible?

Manufacturers must provide particulars on the composition of their products **in a prominent and legible manner,** always using the same print. This applies to catalogues, trade literature and labels.

Information transparency? What about the fact that certain clothes have labels written in a foreign language?

The national authorities may require that their national language(s) be used in the labelling and marking of clothing marketed in their territory. However, they are under no Community obligation to do so.

Not all labels contain particulars on how to look after your clothing, but those that do are sometimes pretty wide of the mark!

At present no Community text regulates this crucial question, although details on how to look after clothes are strongly recommended.

However, manufacturers have entered into voluntary professional agreements to supply you with certain information concerning textile care.

Where can I turn if my purchase is defective or of poor quality?

So the label on your dress does not comply with the legislation in force? Or the quality of your new shirt leaves much to be desired? Remember that as a general rule it is the distributor who is legally liable for the quality of your articles – even in the case of products 'Made in Taiwan' or 'Made in Hong Kong'!

Is there a standard system of sizes?

Well, no. This is for understandable physical reasons – 'types' differ from one country to another and a Dane is not necessarily the same shape as an Italian. So sizes of clothing and shoes are not always the same everywhere. Each country has developed its own measurement system.

The table below gives size equivalents for the United States of America, the United Kingdom and Ireland, and continental Europe. The clothing sizes are approximate but gloves sizes are the same in all countries.

	Men's suits and coats					
United States of America	36	38	40	42	44	46
United Kingdom and Ireland	36	38	40	42	44	46
Continental Europe	46	48	51	54	56	59
Women's suits and dresses						
United States of America	08	10	12	14	16	18
United Kingdom and Ireland	10	12	14	16	18	20
Continental Europe	38	40	42	44	46	48

		Shirts					
United States of America	14	$14 \, ^1/_2$	15	$15 \, ^1/_2$	16	$16 \, ^1/_2$	17
United Kingdom and Ireland	14	$14 \, ^1/_2$	15	$15 \, ^1/_2$	16	$16 \, ^1/_2$	17
Continental Europe	36	37	38	39	41	42	43

	Men's shoes					
United States of America	$7 \, ^1/_2$	8	$8 \, ^1/_2$	$9^1/_2$	$10^1/_2$	$11^1/_2$
United Kingdom and Ireland	7	$7 \, ^1/_2$	8	9	10	11
Continental Europe	$40 \, ^1/_2$	41	42	43	$44 \, ^1/_2$	46

	Women's shoes					
United States of America	6	$6 \, ^1/_2$	7	$7 \, ^1/_2$	8	$8 \, ^1/_2$
United Kingdom and Ireland	$4 \, ^1/_2$	5	$5 \, ^1/_2$	6	$6 \, ^1/_2$	7
Continental Europe	$37 \, ^1/_2$	38	39	$39 \, ^1/_2$	40	$40 \, ^1/_2$

In some garments, you will find labels indicating the sizes in several standards. Indeed some stores provide their clients with correspondence tables of sizes so that you can conveniently switch from one standard to another.

Some hints

Always examine the labels, first when shopping, and then before washing your textiles.

Don't hesitate to take the article back to the store if it turns out to be shoddy. If you fail to receive satisfaction, contact a consumer organization which can tell you how best to proceed.

What remains to be done

Unfortunately, checks by the national authorities on the truthfulness of information contained on labels as to the fibre content of textile products leave much to be desired. For example, a survey by the Italian Consumer Protection Committee revealed that even exclusive, top-of-the range coats and pullovers had a far lower cashmere content than claimed on their labels. The product inspection system in certain countries should be strengthened in order to give full effect to the protection afforded by Community legislation.

Specific sectors

15. Motor cars

Europe of the motor car is moving forward ... on the hard shoulder

In making the internal market for motor vehicles a reality, the European Union has gone through several stages, but the process is not yet complete.

From now on you can buy the car of your choice anywhere in the EU. But you are still obliged:

■ to pay VAT,

■ (in some cases) to pass a roadworthiness test,

■ to have your car registered

in your country of residence. Currently, you may — at your own expense — have to have the vehicle you purchased elsewhere adapted to the technical requirements of your country of residence (roadworthiness).

In a genuine internal market cars will be manufactured according to common technical standards. Hence, there will be no roadworthiness problems when they are being registered.

Specific sectors

Do car prices really differ that much from one country to another?

Yes! The European Commission has found **pre-tax price differentials** between Member States of up to 40% for one and the same model despite the fact that, in a single market, the pre-tax price for cars should be much the same everywhere.

Factors such as exchange rate fluctuations and different specifications for different markets (car radios, electric windows, air conditioning, etc.) account for some of the differential. But the price differences also reflect the commercial policy of the makers who persist in selling their cars at steep prices in certain markets.

The European Commission has entered into discussions with manufacturers with a view to improving the situation.

Nevertheless there remain **differences in tax levels** (VAT, registration tax, special taxes, etc.) which can further inflate the differences between the final prices paid by the consumer. This situation is unlikely to change in the short term, since the national authorities retain their powers of taxation.

 Sellers and prices?

According to the half-yearly Commission survey carried out at the beginning of 1994, Spain is the cheapest EU country for new, tax-free, bottom-of-the-range cars, whereas Italy offers the best bargains for top-of-the-range vehicles.

The same study reveals that France and Germany have the highest average prices.

So is it really worth buying a new car in another country where prices are lower?

While the answer is 'Yes' in principle, in practice things are not quite so clearcut.

You may **encounter quite a number of obstacles** to dissuade you from private or parallel imports. Certain sellers raise their prices for non-resident buyers or simply refuse to deal. Others restrict special offers to their own nationals.

Other abuses noted:

- unreasonable delivery periods;

- demands for excessive down-payments;

- refusal to provide a warranty.

The European Commission is keen to abolish these practices. It has requested all carmakers to ensure that private orders from other countries of the European Union are **dealt with in the same way** as orders placed by normal domestic customers.

Moreover, manufacturers are invited to facilitate price comparison by **regularly publishing lists of recommended prices** for the most popular models and their principal optional extras.

Is it true that VAT on new cars has been lowered?

Harmonization of VAT and excise rates in the European Union has led to a reduction in car prices in certain countries.

However, in practice, the tax reductions have often been offset by an increase in the basic price of the vehicle — in the United Kingdom and Italy for example — or by the creation of a new tax, as in Spain, Belgium and Ireland.

Specific sectors

Can I be sure of finding exactly the same model abroad?

You may be in for the occasional surprise when you buy a car from another country.

Let's take for example the case of a French car: the model sold abroad may be considerably different from the one intended for the French market, **because the basic equipment and optional extras are not necessarily the same.** For example, in Spain, French cars are generally air-conditioned. In France, air conditioning is an option. Hence, before purchasing, **have a good look** at the characteristics of the vehicle you are interested in.

Does one always have to re-register a car purchased abroad?

The Community rules do not authorize you to use, in your country of residence, a car registered abroad. If you are Italian but live in Belgium and are resident there, you will need a Belgian registration plate, no matter where you buy your car.

Again, if you are British and buy a car in Spain to take back to Britain, you will need a UK registration plate.

To obtain it, you must first **pay VAT on your car in your country of residence.** Then you will have to check that your car complies with the technical standards of your country of residence and apply for a roadworthiness certificate. If your car does not satisfy the requirements, like it or not you will have to make the necessary alterations. Once you have the certificate you can proceed with registration.

Things will become simpler as of 1 January 1996 with the introduction of the **Community type-approval procedure.** As of this date, all new models marketed anywhere in the Community will have to comply with common technical standards. The procedure described above will then be obsolete.

What exactly are these technical differences?

Well, the French have a weakness for yellow headlights, the Germans are really into reclining seats and the Italians have a fixation with side-mounted indicators.

Besides there are currently **44 European technical standards** concerning windscreens, brakes, tyres, safety belts, etc. But all these standards considered essential for marketing a given model will not be harmonized until 1996.

 But European anti-pollution standards already exist, if I'm not mistaken.

Yes indeed. These are **standards designed to protect the environment.** Their purpose is to limit exhaust gas emissions, and notably they specify the mandatory use of **catalytic** converters.

All new cars sold since 31 December 1992 must comply with minimum standards concerning carbon monoxide, hydrocarbon and nitrogen oxide emissions.

 And what if I buy a used car?

In this case, ask for written evidence of the transaction (order form, contract, etc.): certain dealers will provide an invoice, but no other document. You should also insist that a deadline for delivery be indicated on the order form.

 New or second hand?

Your car is considered as new — if it has been delivered within six months of manufacture and/or has clocked up less than 6 000 kilometres. In other words, buying a new car does not necessarily mean taking a pristine model straight from the dealer's showrooms. When you buy a new car abroad, the dealer sells it to you tax-free.

Specific sectors

Your car is considered as second hand — if it is over six months old and/or has more than 6 000 kilometres on the clock. In all Member States VAT on second-hand cars is always paid in the country where the vehicle has been purchased, because it is included in the price.

Attention! In certain countries the tax rate differs depending on whether the transaction involves a dealer or just two private parties. In the case of private sales, no tax has to be paid; if a dealer is involved, the tax will be calculated on the basis of the dealer's margin.

 Are there roadworthiness tests in all countries of the European Union?

Periodic roadworthiness tests are mandatory in most countries of the Union, except for Ireland and Portugal.

However, such tests will become **mandatory in all Member States as of 1998** for cars over four years old, and will concern not only safety but also exhaust gas toxicity.

This should make for safer roads and reduce the risk factor in selling used cars abroad.

NB: A second-hand car bought abroad does not have to undergo a roadworthiness test unless the same procedure applies to cars of national origin in the same conditions.

 What if a new car that I bought abroad breaks down?

Don't panic! If your new car breaks down, you will not be left high and dry; the distributors are obliged to honour the warranty.

Remember! **The manufacturer's warranty is valid in all garages in his network,** no matter where in the European Union the vehicle was purchased. So don't hesitate: demand that the work be carried out under warranty by the local manufacturer-approved dealer.

Spare parts — a cautionary word

What about cut-price spare parts that are not approved by the official manufacturer?

Always take a close look at the spare parts and their prices. In some cases these spare parts will have been manufactured by the carmaker or by his official supplier, and so their quality is identical.

Think twice if your car is still under warranty, because certain carmakers disclaim the warranty if your car contains unapproved spare parts.

What about insurance? Can I now insure my car in any Member State?

In theory yes, in practice not yet.

It is now permissible to draw up crossborder contracts relating to compulsory motor vehicle insurance, in accordance with the Community rules, because an insurer may offer services in countries other than the one in which he is established. But the constraints are such that up to now very few companies operate in this way. On the other hand, the owner of the vehicle may not off his own bat look for cheaper insurance abroad (see Chapter 19 on insurance).

And if I have an accident abroad, can I use the 'accident statement' form?

The so-called 'accident statement form' has been drawn up by insurance companies for use throughout the European Union and you may obtain it from your insurance company. It exists in all languages of the Union and its layout is the same for every language so that you and the other driver can fill out the form irrespective of the language he or she speaks.

Specific sectors

Do I have to sit my driving test again when I move abroad?

If you intend moving to another country of the European Union to live there for more than one year, all you have to do is **exchange your national licence for the licence of the Member State in which you wish to reside.** You do not have to sit the test again. But note that each Member State is free to determine the period of validity of its licences.

In 1996 this formality will be abolished and from that date all national licences will have the same Community format. A licence obtained in any country of the European Union will therefore be valid throughout the Community. Bearing in mind that **Finland and Sweden** currently issue driving licences in a credit-card format (although they nevertheless comply with the requirements of the Community model), and likely technological progress in `smart cards' (credit-card sized cards containing a microprocessor), the Commission has just proposed that the Community licence valid for all Member States should offer the choice of either a paper or 'credit card' format.

Moreover, from 1996 onwards, the minimum age for obtaining a licence will be the same throughout the European Community – you will have to be 18 years old to drive a car.

Some hints

If you are considering buying a new or used car abroad, get all the information you can about:

- the price of the model you have in mind (including options) in the country in question;

- equipment (which may differ from one country to another);

- the usual discount;

- down-payments;

- the most advantageous mode of payment (see also Chapter 18 on financial services).

Prepare a list of the documents that the seller should provide you with (invoice, roadworthiness certificate, warranty form, etc.).

In most countries of the European Union the automobile associations and consumer organizations can help you determine what you need; don't hesitate to contact them. Depending on where you live, you may also be able to consult one of the cross-border consumer information centres (see Chapter 3 for their addresses).

Are you moving house? If you want to take your car with you, you will have to have it registered in your new country of residence. It will then be subject to the rules in force concerning such matters as roadworthiness tests, taxation and insurance. Since the systems still vary greatly from one country to another, you are advised to look into the matter thoroughly in advance so as to avoid surprises.

Don't forget that for a number of years yet you will have to exchange your licence for the licence of your new country of residence.

You want to travel abroad? Then stick carefully to the rules of the road — this is the best way to avoid falling foul of the law! Speed limits, maximum blood alcohol, parking regulations, etc. differ from country to country — as do the fines. Before your trip, consult your automobile club or the embassies or tourist offices of your countries of destination.

What remains to be done

Serious barriers to free competition still persist in the car sector which according to consumer advocacy groups impose major extra costs on buyers. These obstacles include:

- authorization for manufacturers to apply exclusive and selective distribution networks (in other words, only authorized dealers may sell cars of a certain make and the manufacturer may require that his dealers do not sell other makes under the same roof);

- the practical difficulties (which are greater in some countries than in others) of buying a car from a foreign-based dealer;

- the lack of competition for spare parts;

- the red tape involved in registering a car purchased abroad.

Ideally, consumers should also be free to buy cars 'inclusive of all taxes' anywhere in the European Union, as is the case for other consumer goods (see Chapter 2 on VAT). However, the exception that applies to new cars (where the buyer pays VAT not in the country of sale but in his country of residence) will not be abolished until 1 January 1997.

As regards car insurance, national markets are only just beginning to open up to foreign competition and the day on which the consumer will be able to take out a policy in another Member State is still a long way away.

16. Travel and tourism

Fewer border checks

Since 26 March 1995, the seven signatories to the Schengen Agreements (the Benelux countries, Germany, France, Spain and Portugal) have abolished all identity checks at their joint borders and strengthened the checks at the borders of the Schengen area.

With effect from that date, therefore, travellers may find three lanes at a port or airport:

- the Schengen lane (at the present time seven Community countries): no checks;
- lanes for other EU citizens (the remaining eight Community countries): the usual identity checks carried out within the European Union;
- non-EU lane: usual identity and customs checks.

... But the traveller is still protected

In the travel sector, consumer protection has long been unequal from one Member State to another. Moreover, travel agencies, which are paid up front for package holidays, have tended to disclaim all liability in the event of problems and to pass the buck to various service providers.

Fortunately, the European Union has forged ahead with legislation affording particular protection to the consumer in the following domains:

- package holidays;
- overbooking of aeroplane seats;
- information provided in travel agencies.

To learn more about these issues and other topics of interest to travellers, follow the guide ...!

Specific sectors

PACKAGE TRIPS

 I like leafing through travel brochures, but sometimes I find the descriptions are too good to be true. Aren't the organizers obliged to tell the truth?

All descriptive information forms part of the contract and hence may not mislead the client through incorrect representation of the service offered.

The organizer is under no legal obligation to provide you with a brochure. But if he does so, none of the information it contains may be misleading. **The descriptive information contained in the brochure is an integral part of the contract.** This means that the organizer or agency is liable if the services provided do not match what is in the brochure.

From now on, **travel agencies may under no circumstances add clauses disclaiming liability** for the inaccuracy of descriptions and photographs.

Whether a brochure has been supplied or not, **the descriptive material** relating to the package trip — including posters, material on display or any advertising material in the travel agencies — **may not contain any misleading information.** This applies both to prices and to all other particulars concerning the trip.

 When I book a package trip, what information does the agency have to provide me with?

A package contract **must be in writing** and must contain detailed particulars concerning the trip, namely:

- destination,

- itinerary,

- accommodation,

- price.

Moreover, you must receive, in due time and in writing, the following additional information:

- information on passport and visa requirements;

- health formalities (vaccines, etc.);

- times and places of intermediate stops and transport connections;

- detailed particulars on accommodation *en route* (for example, in trains or boats);

- the name, address and telephone number of the organization or agency's local representative;

- information on the optional conclusion of an insurance policy to cover the cost of cancellation or the cost of assistance, including repatriation, in the event of accident or illness.

Can the organizer alter the price of my trip?

The prices mentioned in your contract may not be revised, unless there are changes in transport costs, taxes or the exchange rate. At any rate, the contract must specifically mention the possibility of revision, as well as the precise modalities for calculating the proper price.

At any rate, **during the 20 days prior to departure** the initial price cannot be raised, even for the abovementioned reasons.

If, for example, I am prevented from travel for family reasons, can I find a replacement?

If you are prevented from proceeding with the package, **you can always transfer your booking to a person of your choice,** provided they satisfy the conditions required for participation (visa, passport, etc.).

Specific sectors

In the event of failure to perform the contract, who is ultimately liable?

Liability for proper performance of the contract must be clearly specified in national legislation. Liability may lie with the **tour operator** or the **travel agency:** consult a consumer organization or the responsible ministry for further details beforehand.

Note that the person or organization in question is strictly liable for any failure to perform the contract.

 What security do I have if the organizer goes bust, or in the event of changes to or shortcomings in the contract?

The organizer must provide sufficient evidence of security. Hence, if he goes bankrupt before your departure or during your stay, you have to be fully refunded or repatriated without extra cost.

Guarantee systems/solvency insurance exist in several countries to help you. These systems are organized either voluntarily by the travel agencies or under the control of the national authorities.

If your contract is altered or improperly performed, you are free to cancel it without incurring penalties and, in certain cases, you are entitled to damages or to a refund of the money paid over. The organizer may propose alternative solutions.

 This protection applies to package trips, but does it also apply if I merely ask my travel agency to sell me a plane ticket, for example?

The protection afforded by Community legislation covers only package trips and does not apply to isolated services, such as simply booking a hotel, or buying a ticket, without any other service.

A package means the pre-arranged combination of no fewer than two of the following:

- transport;

- accommodation;

- other tourist services not ancillary to transport or accommodation and accounting for a significant proportion of the package,

when the service covers a period of 24 hours or includes overnight accommodation and is sold at an inclusive price.

 Does this legislation apply if I take a holiday organized by a holiday club?

Yes! You are protected provided the trip falls within the definition of a package set out above.

NB: Separate billing of various components of the same package does not absolve the organizer or retailer of his obligations.

DENIED BOARDING ON FLIGHTS

 My airline refused to let me board the plane because it had made more reservations than there were seats available. What can I do?

Overbooking of airplane seats is a recurrent problem in Europe. Carriers sell more tickets than there are seats on the plane, counting on a certain percentage of no-shows.

Did you present yourself in time at the check-in desk? Is your ticket still valid and has your reservation been confirmed? In the event of overbooking, you are entitled to

Specific sectors

immediate financial compensation, in the form of travel vouchers or cash.

The amount of compensation is **ECU 150** for flights of up to 3 500 km, while for flights of more than 3 500 km you are entitled to up to **ECU 300**. However, these sums may be halved if the next flight is available within two or four hours respectively.

Apart from paying this compensation, the company must reroute you to your destination on the next available flight. You are always free to opt for a refund of the price of your ticket.

 And who foots the bill if I have to kill time at the airport?

Telephone calls, faxes, accommodation, meals and refreshments — **all outgoings which can be normally justified must be met by the air carrier,** while you're waiting for the next available flight.

COMPUTERIZED RESERVATION SYSTEMS: FULL, IMPARTIAL AND OBJECTIVE INFORMATION

 How can I learn about the fares applied by the different air carriers for the same journey?

The air carriers must provide the travel agencies which use their computerized reservation services to reserve your tickets with information on all available flights (times, fares, number of seats, etc.). Clear, comprehensible data that are impartial in their presentation and identical for all airports and flights relating to the same itinerary must be presented.

Moreover, all personal information (date of birth, address, etc.) which you may communicate to a travel agency must remain confidential.

MOTOR VEHICLE INSURANCE

Am I insured if I travel by car in another Member State?

In European law consumers enjoy third-party coverage in the country visited, without having to pay any additional premiums.

But **remember:** it is often useful to sign a contract of assistance on the lines offered by the automobile clubs, which are relatively inexpensive, if only to be covered in the event of a breakdown or illness. In certain countries, if you are involved in a car accident, the authorities may require you to lodge a security pending the allocation of fault. So make sure that your contract includes a 'security-guarantee' (see Chapter 19 on insurance).

SHOPPING WHILE ON HOLIDAY

Are there still restrictions on shopping in other countries of the European Union?

No. You are now free to buy as much as you like, **provided the goods are intended for your personal consumption** and provided you have paid your taxes in the country of purchase.

Free movement of goods applies even to alcohol, tobacco and perfumes, again provided you don't overdo it and provided that they are for your personal use. Customs officers are entitled to ask a few questions if you are carrying more than:

- 800 cigarettes,

- 90 litres of wine,

- 110 litres of beer or

- 10 litres of spirits.

Naturally, these quantities are illustrative only, because, for example, if your daughter is about to marry and you are organizing the reception, you are perfectly entitled to take larger quantities.

At any rate, don't forget that **taxes and excise** (normally this concerns only VAT) have to be paid in the country of purchase at the local rate. It is up to you to check whether cross-border shopping is worth it (for further information, see Chapter 1 'Shopping abroad').

 ... and what about duty-free purchases?

When you travel within the European Union, you are still entitled to purchase in duty-free shops in airports and ports **until 30 June 1999.**

After this date, duty-free shops will be restricted to travellers entering or leaving the Community. This means that you will not be able to shop in the duty-free when travelling, say, from Paris to Athens.

Duty-free purchases are and will remain **strictly regulated:** the quantities of products sold are limited per person and per trip. Information on these limits is to be found in the duty-free shops.

HEALTH

 What if I fall ill while on holiday?

A person travelling in another Member State of the European Union can use the public health services of the host country in accordance with the reimbursement arrangements applicable under the legislation of the host country. This system operates thanks to a system of clearing houses linking the sickness insurance schemes of the various countries of the Union.

In order to prove entitlement to health care in the traveller's home country, he or she must hand over to the health care institution an 'E 111' form (or a similar form for an unemployed or retired person, for example) obtainable in your home country before you go abroad. It is a good idea to ask your social security office what form you need.

If you do not have the E 111 form, you will have to wait patiently until you return home to get your refund.

Some hints

Get informed! Member State Governments are legally obliged to transpose Community law on package trips; hence, ask a consumer organization whether your national legislation faithfully reflects the requirements of the Community text.

Invoke your rights: when you buy a package holiday, always ask for a written contract and check that it is just what you want. If you are denied boarding on a scheduled flight although your reservation is in order, immediately ask for the compensation which is your due.

If necessary complain: if you think your rights have been violated, write to a consumers' advisory service or to the appropriate consultative body. If you do not get satisfaction, address the Ministry concerned or your national or European MP.

Cheap travel for the young (and the not so young) in Europe

Many carriers grant fare reductions, provided certain conditions are fulfilled – date or time of journey, season, duration of stay, age, etc. It is worth checking because there are big potential savings (up to 50%).

Specific sectors

What remains to be done

Under Community law travellers are definitely better protected than they were some years ago.

And remember: legislation in certain Member States is even more friendly to travellers. For example, in the United Kingdom missing or inadequate information constitutes an offence!

However, you may be in for an uphill struggle when trying to pin down liability for package trips. In certain Member States, such as France, the travel agents consider that it is the supplier who is liable in the event of failure to deliver (for example the hotel owner).

Moreover, if a package trip is cancelled, you will have no redress if this is due to there being an insufficient number of participants or to *force majeure*.

17. Housing (including timeshares)

Because of its economic and social significance, the housing market has long been subject to specific rules at national and sometimes regional level.

The free movement of persons and capital in the European Union has increased the demand for housing on the part of non-residents.

This trend has turned the spotlight on certain practices in the housing sector which are prejudicial to consumers' interests or which constitute barriers to the freedom to provide services. More specifically, the relatively new formula of 'immovable property on a timeshare basis' — or timeshares — has been the source of many complaints.

Do I really have the right to go and live in another country of the European Union?

Yes! Every citizen of the European Union has the right to go and live in another country of the Union, without being subject to any discrimination on the grounds of his nationality.

 And as a new resident, am I also entitled to buy property?

Yes, as a rule, because the right to housing — rented or purchased — is a prerequisite to the right of residence.

However, the real estate market is not subject to Community rules and some countries such as Austria, Denmark, Finland, Greece and Italy impose restrictions on the purchase of property by citizens from other countries of the European Union.

If you want to buy property, you are well advised **to take an expert's advice,** because legislation, practices and costs differ considerably from one country to another. For example, in Belgium, the transaction costs are pretty steep (approximately 16% of the purchase price) and hence there is no point in buying a house unless you intend to stay in the country for several years. On the other hand, in the United Kingdom, where transaction costs are far lower and rented accommodation is more difficult to come by, it may be worth buying a house even if you only want to stay for one or two years.

 But to buy property I would have to transfer my savings — do I need an authorization?

No! The single market also includes **the free movement of capital.** This means that when you go to live in another Member State you are entitled to take your savings with you or to transfer them.

In certain countries the banks still ask you to set out the reasons for international transfers but as a rule this information is intended for statistical purposes only and is not equivalent to a request for an authorization.

Take care! Bank charges for international transfers may be quite high. Check them out before going ahead with the transaction. See also Chapter 18 on financial services.

If I don't have enough put by to buy the villa of my dreams, can I get a mortgage in my new country of residence?

In the European Union, the principle of non-discrimination on the basis of nationality is fundamental. Hence, if you satisfy the same conditions that nationals of the country must meet to obtain a mortgage, the credit institution is not entitled to turn you down on the grounds of your nationality.

However, in practice banks are reluctant to grant mortgages to people whose main residence or sources of in-come are abroad. In general, banks consider that these loans are too risky or are only willing to grant them in conjunction with securities or premiums that make the deal uninteresting.

Consult financial organizations about the proposed conditions and, moreover, ask for advice from a consumer organization in the country in question.

Look before you leap because conditions for loans vary considerably from one country to another and here again an expert's advice can make all the difference.

How can I compare the cost of different loan offers? Are calculations made on the same basis as in my country of origin?

Community law on consumer credit lays down a single formula for calculating the total cost of credit, in order to facilitate comparison between different offers.

Although **this legislation does not yet apply to mort-**

Specific sectors

gages, certain countries (such as Austria, Germany, Finland, France and Ireland) nonetheless stipulate a single formula for calculating the total cost of a mortgage.

Again, useful information and advice may be had from consumer organizations in the country in question, or from the cross-border consumer information centres.

 If I move abroad, can I take my furniture and personal effects with me?

In general, when you move house, you are entitled to take your furniture and other goods, without paying tax, provided they are intended for your personal use. There are exceptions concerning the importation of domestic animals to the United Kingdom and Ireland, for veterinary health reasons.

 I've heard that it is possible to 'purchase the right to use' a flat as a holiday residence for one or several weeks per year. However, my neighbour warned me to be careful because there are so many swindlers in the market. What do you think?

Certain firms specialize in selling what are known as **timeshares**.

By means of a 'timeshare', private individuals can 'purchase' the right to use holiday accommodation for one or more weeks each year over quite a long period (20 years for example). They may also be entitled to exchange their entitlement and hence may **in principle** freely alter the dates and location of their holiday.

As you may know, timeshares have been the source of **much controversy**, primarily because of the absence of legal protection.

However, there are in the timeshare sector **a certain number of reliable firms!** Indeed it is these firms that have been urging the Community authorities to regulate the sector on the grounds that the abuses committed by rogue operators have injured consumers and given a bad name to an investment which, initially, was not such a bad idea.

 But how can one recognize swindlers?

Some developers are past masters in pressure selling techniques and at pulling the wool over your eyes. You cannot be vigilant enough, because — or so it seems — what the developers promise and what you actually get are still poles apart.

These developers have a whole ragbag of selling techniques: questionnaires hurriedly filled in at a street corner, pseudo-surveys, telephone selling, lotteries or competitions, to mention but a few.

 What are the most frequent difficulties that arise with timeshares?

Firstly, there is **the choice of words.** Contracts relating to the purchase of the right to use immovable properties on a timeshare basis are generally called timeshare contracts but a variety of other designations are also used and so it is not always easy to know precisely what you are letting yourself in for. Are you a co-owner? Do you have the right to lease the property for a particular period? Have you purchased shares in a **property** firm? Everything hinges on the wording!

Further particulars in the contract concern supplementary charges, which have a tendency to proliferate:

- very high down-payments;

- dossier handling charges;

- annual management fees;

- charges that increase over time (such as maintenance costs);

- the exchange pool is not free of charge.

Timeshares may be difficult to resell: in many cases it may be difficult to sell your property, even for a derisory sum! Sad to say, many of these residences deteriorate very rapidly, so many owners resign themselves to letting them out.

To crown it all, national legislation is far from simple:

- In **France,** you're not considered as the owner but as someone who is entitled to use a flat for a determined and regular period. French law considers that you are an 'associate' to a private company providing you with various services.

- **In Portugal** you are a true owner. This is a real and established right.

- In **Greece,** timesharing is almost equivalent to 'multiple renting'. This formula is used because it does confer upon you the title of owner. In reality, you will be renting your holiday week for the rest of your life!

- In the **United Kingdom,** welcome to the club. Here, timeshares often take the form of a trustee club, which you are required to join. Payment of the membership fee entitles you to use the facilities of a firm which is affiliated in some way to the club.

Thus it is often difficult to know what law applies and what legislation protects you if something goes wrong. One example which is by no means far-fetched: a **German** firm selling **Spanish** timeshares to **British** citizens – even lawyers throw up their hands at the thought!

 Well, it's time for the European Union to do something!

Perfectly right! To combat this growth in confidence rackets and the uncertainty of national legislation, the European Union has taken the initiative by legislating in the field of timeshares.

But beware! This legislation will not enter into force until April 1997.

 What kind of protection does this legislation offer?

Broadly, this text introduces the following forms of protection:

- More clearly defined terms: a 'timeshare' is defined as the `purchase of a right to utilize one or several immovable properties on a timeshare basis'.

- A written contract: the seller must always provide a written contract, drafted in the language of your country of residence or your own mother tongue — whichever you prefer — provided that it is one of the official languages of the European Union.

- A brochure forming part of the contract: information on the conditions underlying the transaction and the product must be as complete as possible; notably, the seller must provide you with written information prior to signature of the contract (of which this information is an integral part). Otherwise the contract is null and void.

- An address and articles of association: the name, address and legal status of the seller at the time of conclusion of the contract must be set out in the document to be signed, failing which the contract is null and void and in which case you are perfectly entitled to refuse to make payment, even if you have signed.

- Transparency of the figures: the total price to be paid must be set out in your contract. It must include charges for the right to use the facilities and joint services, mandatory legal fees and management fees.

Specific sectors

- Guarantees: the draft also provides that Member States must establish guarantees:

  - if the immovable property is still under construction;

  - in the event of the seller's failure to perform the services promised.

- The possibility of repudiating the contract: you will have a 10-day cooling-off period during which you can back out of the contract without incurring any penalty, after signature of the contract.

- Greater legal protection: you cannot be deprived of the protection accorded to you by this Community legislation, even if the applicable law mentioned in the contract is that of a non-Community country.

- Economic protection: the seller cannot demand down payments during the cooling-off period. Be particularly careful on this point.

- Moreover, if you have signed a credit contract with a financial institution in order to purchase a timeshare and you then rescind the timeshare contract, you also have the right to rescind the credit contract.

This European initiative sets out the minimum protection to which consumers in all countries of the European Union are entitled. The national authorities may adopt more stringent measures if they think there is a need for them.

Some hints

Regarding timeshares:
In this field, we are currently in a transitional period between adoption of European legislation and its enactment as part of the various European legislations. Until national legislation based on the European provisions actu-

ally comes into force, you must therefore bear in mind that the only legislation that protects you is that in force in the country where the timeshare concerned is located.

So far, only four countries (France, Portugal, the United Kingdom and Greece) have an active statute to protect you against the sharp practices of certain firms.

This means, for example, that irrespective of your nationality you are protected by French legislation if you sign a timeshare contract in France. By contrast, if you decide to buy a life-time holiday in a country other than these four, there is no specific legislation setting out what has to be done in the event of a dispute. The other Member States are patiently awaiting the adoption of Community legislation on timeshares before taking action themselves.

Therefore:
Insist on as many guarantees as possible: it is better to be prudent than to put your faith in procedural remedies. While certain Member States have introduced rapid claims procedures, others require endless litigation.

Avoid taking ill-considered risks: insist on certain terms being en-

tered into your contract. Insist on examining this document carefully before signing it!

Collect as much information as possible and if you have a problem don't hesitate to consult your consumer association. Real estate confederations specialized in selling tourist accommodation can also help. Certain European timeshare organizations have an excellent knowledge of firms specialized in this domain and will be able to fill you in. In some cases they may be able to intervene directly *vis-à-vis* professionals.

Given that we are in a transitional period, Community legislation is probably not yet in force in all Member States and so we advise you to consult your consumer association for information on the legal situation in the various Member States.

In general:
As regards real estate transactions, remember that the more information and advice you obtain the better.

Don't forget that this type of transaction raises an abundance of related problems such as:

• taxation law;

• insurance;

Specific sectors

- mortgages and registration of real estate;

- building permits;

- technical inspections of buildings;

- the law of inheritance.

What remains to be done

Since the European legislation will not be applicable in all Member States until April 1997, the protection offered by timeshare legislation will apply only from that date.

As in the case of many other classes of cross-border transactions, consumers who have to resolve a dispute relating to housing often face legal difficulties and complex and costly procedures. Hence it is vital to improve access to justice for consumers.

18. Financial services

One of the cornerstones of the single market is **the free movement of capital.**

What this means is that there are no longer any restrictions on the transfer of money from one Community country to another. In principle you can:

■ keep your money where you want to;

■ transfer your money wherever you want to and

■ borrow money wherever it suits you best.

At present the costs of purchasing foreign currency and of bank transfers between countries of the European Union are barriers that prevent consumers from making the most of the single financial market. Let us hope that competition will motivate banks to offer you better quality services at lower prices.

Obviously, only the introduction of the ecu as a single currency in everyday transactions will definitively solve the problem of fluctuating exchange rates.

While awaiting better times, it is better to do your sums and take whatever advice you can get.

Since there is no single currency, how can I pay for my purchases when I go shopping abroad within the Union?

You have several options:

- Firstly, you can pay for your purchases **in cash;** however, there are certain drawbacks in using cash, one being the risk of theft. You will also lose out if you do not spend all your foreign currency and so have to convert it back again.

- Another popular form of payment is the **Eurocheque** system. The big advantage here is that the charges are fixed and that you know what they are in advance. However, there is a ceiling on these cheques and this may be bothersome if you want to buy something costly.

- You can also use your **credit card or payment card,** especially if this card is part of a well-known network such as Visa, Mastercard or American Express. The attraction here is that you can avoid all the hassle associated with changing money and can even take advantage of favourable rates. However, the associated costs can be quite steep.

- The safest method is probably the **international transfer,** via a bank or a post office. The drawbacks here are the charges involved, which may be high — especially if you want to transfer a modest sum through a bank — and the time it takes for the money to arrive. A similar method is to use a cheque guaranteed by a bank.

 If I want to buy foreign currency, where is the best place to do so?

Consult the exchange rates in the press and compare them with those offered by the banks and bureaux de change. This is worth the trouble because there are often differences between the rates offered by these financial institutions.

At any rate, get information on the exchange rate, the commission and any other charges associated with the operation.

Beware of bureaux de change which go in for aggressive publicity and, for example, assure you that they charge no commission. Check whether the proposed rate is really interesting, and inquire about supplementary charges. Finally, always ask for a receipt clearly setting out all details of the operation.

 And if I want to pay by cheque or card?

For years the Community has been working hard to facilitate the use of cards and cheques beyond the national frontiers. The aim is to improve the efficiency, speed and reliability of these payment systems and to reduce their costs, which are often excessive. Several recommendations have been addressed to the banks and some progress has been made, notably the acceptance by cash dispensers of cards issued in another country.

Other recommendations concern **a European code of conduct relating to electronic payment and contracts between cardholders and card issuers.** However, in the absence of binding measures, progress to date has been unsatisfactory, notably as regards reducing costs.

In practice, in several countries of the European Union, consumers use Eurocheques with a guarantee card to pay in shops, restaurants, etc. This payment system is particularly widespread in Germany and the Benelux countries, cheques of this kind being accepted practically everywhere, unless the sum is very small. However, normal bank cheques or post office cheques are rarely accepted in shops, restaurants and hotels in other countries.

Specific sectors

Payments by **card** such as Visa, Eurocard/Mastercard, American Express and Diners Club, for which a special invoice has to be signed, are becoming increasingly popular in shops throughout the European Union. However, a BEUC (European Bureau of Consumers' Unions) study claims that there are considerable differences between countries — apparently, these cards are particularly popular in France, the United Kingdom and Spain. Countries also differ in their willingness to accept particular cards. For example, Visa cards are welcomed in France, the United Kingdom and Spain but are less well established in Germany and Italy; Eurocard/Mastercard is also popular in France, Spain and the United Kingdom, but less useful in Ireland and Denmark.

Electronic payment by bank card in shops, for which you use a personal access code, is still largely limited to national usage. So don't rely on this system of payment when you go abroad.

 ### *What rights do I have when I use a credit card?*

For the moment, there are no strict rules governing the issue and use of credit cards and payment cards. However, the European Union has issued recommendations and you are keenly urged to compare the conditions of use offered to you with those recommended.

Briefly, the **recommended conditions** are as follows:

- each card issuer must draw up full and fair terms of contract in writing;

- the contract must indicate that the holder shall not be financially liable after notifying theft or loss of his card, provided he complies with the provisions of the contract and has not acted negligently or fraudulently;

- in the event of a dispute, the burden of proof lies with the card issuer, who must show that the operation was accurately recorded and entered into the accounts and was not affected by technical breakdown or other deficiency;

■ the holder of the card has a right to be supplied with a record of his operations;

■ the card issuer must provide the holder with the possibility of notifying loss or theft within 24 hours, using a system that can be accessed at any time of the day or night;

■ pending notification of theft or loss, the cardholder's liability is limited to **ECU 150.** This liability is terminated on notification, except where the holder has acted with extreme negligence or fraudulently.

But remember: a Community recommendation is in no way binding!

Can I use a card or cheques to withdraw money from banks, post offices and cash dispensers when I am abroad?

It is becoming increasingly possible to withdraw cash from cash dispensers or to cash a cheque abroad. But be careful! Conditions of access and use depend on the country and the card or cheque used.

As regards **cash dispensers,** you will have to find one which accepts your card. Therefore, before your departure, ask for the list of addresses approved by your card issuer and for details on costs. Note also that dispensers are not equally widespread in all countries and that Eurocheque cards can also be used to withdraw notes from cash dispensers.

If you have **postal cheques** you can withdraw money at all post offices, except for Germany, Ireland and the United Kingdom, where only some post offices provide this service. **Eurocheques** are welcomed by most banks, except in Ireland, Denmark and Portugal.

Specific sectors

The possibilities of withdrawing cash from banks using a card also differ. Most banks in Spain and Italy, for example, accept Visa cards and Eurocard/Mastercards but you may have far more difficulty in finding a bank that will agree to such transactions in Greece or in Belgium.

 What do these operations cost, and what are my rights?

According to studies conducted by several consumer associations, costs of payment operations performed abroad are often impossible to determine in advance because of the lack of transparency or even the total failure of the card issuers and banks to provide users with information.

 And what if I want to transfer money from my bank account to a bank account I have opened in another country? Is this more advantageous?

For the present, the cost of international bank transfers are very lacking in transparency and often disproportionate. According to a 1993 study, the cost of transferring ECU 100 ranges from ECU 14 to 43. While the time taken to perform such transactions was generally satisfactory, in some cases there were unacceptable delays.

Moreover, certain banks have the habit of slapping on 'a double deduction', i.e. they charge both the issuer of the order and the beneficiary. Finally, these bank operations are not always reliable, many transfers never arriving at their destination.

The Commission has accordingly recently decided to draft legislation to cover this situation. Once the legislation has been passed, banks will be required to keep costs to a certain level and to respect minimum deadlines as a way of improving service to consumers. Moreover, they will be required to keep consumers properly informed about these transfers.

And does the same apply to transfers by post?

International postal orders are at least as reliable and indeed the services offered by the postal authorities are often better value than those provided by the banks. If you frequently have to transfer money to another country in the Union, you would be well advised to open a postal cheque account. Today, most European post offices offer this service, except in Greece, Ireland and Portugal. The new Eurogiro system is an electronic payment system which is particularly fast, advantageous and easy to access, because anyone can use it. The beneficiary's account is credited within three days.

Moreover, in most Member States the post offices have a network of automatic cash dispensers which you can use both at home and abroad. You can also use your card or your postal cheques in foreign post offices to withdraw cash from your account.

Does that mean that I can open a bank account or postal account anywhere in the European Union?

Certainly, that goes without saying in the single market, whether you are of Greek, Italian or Dutch or any other Community nationality.

Naturally, there is some red tape: hence, to open an account in Spain, for example, non-resident European citizens must present a 'negative residence permit' issued by the police.

I've often heard of the ecu but what use is it to consumers?

As a precursor to a single currency, more widespread use of the ecu would make much of this chapter obsolete — hence, consumers would no longer have to compare exchange rates, or to pay commissions when purchasing foreign currency.

Even now it is possible to conduct a certain number of

Specific sectors

operations denominated in ecus, such as opening an account, making certain investments, obtaining travellers cheques, etc.

But **be careful!** Since the ecu is still considered to be a foreign currency, converting your national currency into ecus normally involves charges. So, keep abreast of things!

 Can I transfer my money freely from one Member State to another or are there still restrictions?

In principle, money has been free to circulate throughout the Union since 1990. Hence you are completely free to make or receive payments from and to anywhere in the Community. The few remaining restrictions, notably in Greece and Portugal, are to be phased out by 1995.

However, in certain countries there will be tax formalities to be complied with. Hence in France, a customs declaration is indispensable for sums in excess of FF 50 000. In Spain, you have to make a declaration when you import or export between PTA 1 and 5 million, while an administrative authorization is required if you want to export more than PTA 5 million from the country.

 So I can invest my savings in the country offering the highest interest rates?

This is possible, but beware! Whether this is worth the bother depends on more factors than the interest rate. A lot depends on what you want to do with the money later, and in what country. So, get advice.

 The BCCI scandal, where a bank became insolvent and lots of people lost their savings, really scared me. Are there no controls on bank solvency?

The BCCI bankruptcy showed the need to guarantee consumers a common level of legal protection against loss of their deposits in the event of a bank's becoming insolvent.

European legislation says that in principle, and with effect from July 1995, national authorities must guarantee all depositers a right of reimbursement of up to 20 000 ecus should a bank become insolvent. **Warning!** In certain countries, the ceiling for reimbursement will remain limited to 15 000 ecus until 1999.

However, most countries have established deposit-guarantee schemes, although the scope and **level of legal protection differs considerably from one country to another.**

The European Commission has also proposed measures for more stringent surveillance of banks and credit institutions within the EU: the head office of a branch should be located in the same country as that of the registered office, so that the competent authorities can police it effectively. The external experts responsible for auditing the accounts should also notify the authorities of any facts likely to endanger the bank's existence or to imperil the protection of the depositors.

Can I get a loan anywhere in Europe?

Yes! But be careful: you may also sacrifice benefits and advantageous conditions associated with certain loans, because of exchange rate fluctuations or variations in the rates.

NB: Housing loans with variable rates and repayment periods are very commonplace in the United Kingdom. Belgium, Germany and the Netherlands have loans with renegotiable rates. In Spain and Portugal, the rates are indexed.

In general it is difficult to determine precisely in advance the real cost of a loan. Again, since you have to settle your repayments abroad, there is every likelihood — if one may say so — of your having to pay supplementary charges for cross-border transfers.

Specific sectors

And a further word of warning: Community legislation on consumer credit will not apply to disputes **if the amount borrowed is less than 200 ecus or more than 20 000 ecus!**

 How can I compare interest rates on loans in different countries?

Under Community legislation, you have the right to a **written contract,** which must state:

- the annual percentage rate of charge (APR);

- the total amount to be repaid, as well as the number and frequency of repayments.

Loan offers must mention **the annual percentage rate of charge,** which is calculated not only on the basis of the interest to be paid but also certain other charges linked to the loan and which therefore reflects the real cost of your credit.

From 1 January 1996 at the latest, this calculation will be conducted using a comparable formula in all countries of the EU. Hence you will from then on have a 'yardstick' for making the best possible choice.

Warning! Mortgages are not covered by European legislation except in those countries where legislation covering them already exists.

However, **as regards such loans,** you are still protected under the law of the country in which you take out the mortgage. This is because the national authorities are free to enact more stringent domestic measures to ensure a higher level of protection for consumers.

 What are my rights when I take out a consumer loan?

You can seek redress if a bank fails to observe the rules governing consumer credit. Hence, in the event of a dispute, you have every right to bring an action against the lender, either by addressing your national authorities or by contacting a supervisory agency (such as a mediator).

Since 'prevention is better than cure', in certain countries lenders and providers of credit have to possess a licence and such financial establishments are closely monitored.

Some hints

So you want to buy the fitted kitchen of your dreams? But you would like to borrow money to pay for it. Look before you leap! Here are some tips which we hope will enable you to steer clear of certain pitfalls.

Firstly, insist on an offer in writing. Before signing a credit contract, ask the lender to provide you with a written proposal. Make sure that it contains the following particulars:

- name and address of the lender;

- your name and address;

- name of the goods or service purchased;

- price;

- the credit sum;

- the interest rate (APR);

- the conditions under which this rate can be revised;

- duration of the loan;

- number of repayments and their amounts.

Your contract should also indicate the dates on which the repayments have to be made, along with the total amount, including interest and miscellaneous costs.

Again, sit back and think! Take the time to peruse your contract again. Many people are unaware that in certain countries, such as France, Belgium, and Germany, at this stage in the deal you still have a cooling-off period. So ask around.

Before returning your signed contract to the seller, ensure that all the sections have been correctly filled in and that the proposal bears the date of your signature. And carefully guard your own copy of the contract. It may always come in useful.

Never sign a blank contract, cheque, form, etc.

Specific sectors

What remains to be done

Consumers stand to gain less from the completion of the single market than the banks as long as simple cross-border banking transactions, such as money transfers or payment by cheque remain extremely burdensome and time-consuming. Moreover, consumers are not informed beforehand of the costs or delays, because of lack of transparency.

The banks have not applied the 1988 and 1990 recommendations concerning payment systems and transparency of costs respectively. They have preferred to draw up their own codes of conduct. The European Commission has undertaken to draft legislation to deal with this problem but its proposals have not yet been discussed by the ministers representing the Member States.

It is difficult to compare mortgage costs, given that there is no common rule for calculating the annual rate of interest (see also Chapter 17 on housing).

Bank deposit guarantees are not yet governed by common rules throughout the European Union. Such rules exist in some Member States but not in others.

19. Insurance

Europe-wide insurance: reassuring or not?

In its agenda for building the internal market, the European Union gives high priority to the free movement of services, including insurance.

In principle, since July 1994, private individuals may take out life assurance or non-life assurance policies in any Community Member State.

Hence consumers will have a wider choice both as regards the terms of the policies offered to them and the prices offered by the various European insurance companies.

Specific sectors

I own a flat on the Costa Brava: can I have it insured in my own country just as in Spain?

Since July 1994 you may take out a package policy for your second home **with the company of your choice in any country of the European Union.**

The freedom to provide insurance services applies also to non-life assurance, such as civil liability, supplementary sickness insurance, etc.

 If I take out an insurance policy abroad, do I have the same rights as at home in implementing my insurance contract?

No! **Contract law differs from one country to another.** Hence, ideally you should be familiar with the foreign law that applies to your contract. And this is no easy matter. No doubt this partly explains why consumers have been less than keen on the idea. If you don't know what exactly a contract implies, there is always the risk of hassle at some later stage.

However, **Community legislation protects you against unfair terms** in contracts.

 Can I also take out life assurance in another country?

By all means! Freedom to provide services means that you are quite free to take out **life assurance** by directly contacting a company of your choice that is established and approved in another Member State.

There are two possible scenarios: either you of your own accord contact an insurer or an agent established in a country other than the one in which you reside; the contract will then be subject to financial control by the insurer's head office.

Alternatively, the company approaches you. In this case the contract is signed at the initiative of the firm. It is then subject to tax inspection in your country of residence.

In both cases the company must provide you with all information concerning the scope and conditions of the insurance policy. Moreover, you have a right to repudi-ate the contract within a **cooling-off period** of 14 to 30 days. This period begins to run from the moment the company informs you that your contract has been concluded. During this period, you may back out of the contract.

NB: In Belgium, all **life assurance policies** are null and void if the law applicable to the contract is not Belgian law.

Can I take out car insurance in another country?

Yes, as of 1 July 1994, you can have your car insured with any car insurance company in any EU country.

Naturally, you should **compare the prices and terms of the policy** in the different countries. As to **coverage,** each country has its own rules.

As regards car insurance, you should be aware that **your insurer cannot require that you pay a supplement** to en-sure that your third-party policy covers you throughout the Community. The guarantee automatically applies to the entire territory of the Community and so your premium cannot be raised for this reason.

NB: In Belgium and in the Netherlands you can only regis-ter your car if the law applicable to your **car insurance** contract is Belgian or Netherlands law respectively.

Where are the prices for car insurance policies most competitive?

In some cases car insurance premiums differ considerably between one country and another depending on the vehicle's technical specifications, its age and the driver's claims history as well as the nature of the risk.

Specific sectors

These differences, which are mainly reflected in the 'bonus-malus' scales, are likely to become even greater because the insurance companies now have greater leeway following deregulation. Hence, **keep informed** to be sure that you have the most up-to-date data.

Moreover, insurance premiums also depend on taxes. Taxes vary greatly from one country to another. For example, Denmark has higher tax rates for insuring private individuals (50%) than France (33%), or the United Kingdom (0%).

 If I have a traffic accident abroad, am I always covered by my car insurance policy?

Like all European car insurance policies, your contract provides coverage only in regard to your civil liability for physical injury and damage to property in any country of the European Union.

This guarantee also covers all the other passengers in your vehicle, whether the accident happens at home or elsewhere in the Community.

 I understand. But what guarantees do I have?

All mandatory third-party motor vehicle insurance policies provide for minimum compensation in the event of an accident. This minimum coverage is the same (in terms of ecus) in all countries or almost!

Currently, minimum coverage in most countries is ECU 350 000 for physical injury and ECU 100 000 for damage to property.

However, certain countries — specifically Greece, Spain and Portugal — have not yet laid down minimum sums to be paid in the event of an accident. These countries are obliged to fall in line by 1 January 1996.

The amount due to you is paid by the **national motor vehicle insurers' bureau** of the country in which the accident occurred. Currently, each country has its own bureau for settling accidents.

And if I am involved in an accident caused by somebody who was uninsured?

Fortunately, Community legislation covers this eventuality: in such cases a **guarantee fund** will come to your rescue. This also applies in the case of hit and run accidents.

Likewise, you are always entitled to compensation if the vehicle was driven by an unauthorized person or somebody who does not hold a driving licence; again, you are covered if the owner has failed to comply with roadworthiness test requirements. Indeed the waivers mentioned in certain contracts and which are known as 'exclusion clauses' **in no way affect the victim's rights.** This means that the insurer cannot refuse to pay damages on the pretext that one or other of these situations applies to you.

But note: drunken drivers are deprived of all coverage in France, Belgium, Germany and Spain.

To be prepared for all such eventualities, you are keenly urged to **take out a legal aid policy.** To avoid a conflict of interest when this coverage is included in the main insurance policy, Community legislation provides that the legal aid policy must be distinct from the main insurance policy and that the policyholder must have the right to choose his own legal representation freely.

Specific sectors

Some hints

Taking out insurance abroad? Before going ahead, compare the situation in your own country with the situation abroad in terms of guarantees, prices, etc. Consider carefully the costs and additional effort involved in taking out insurance policies in another country.

First, ask yourself a number of questions:

Is the insurance company you are dealing with licensed to propose contracts with private individuals?

Do you have enough information to compare the guarantees?

How will you be compensated? What is your own personal liability threshold?

Does the premium include taxes?

In the event of an accident, who do you turn to? And what language is to be used?

Ask for references! Have you been solicited by a foreign company and would like to take out the policy they have proposed? Consult your national advisory authorities and ask for the company's references.

Always ask for a version of your contract drafted in your own language. The same goes for all other documents they send you.

The facts of the law: find out what law will be applicable to your contract and the place of jurisdiction in the event of a dispute. If the applicable law is not that of your own country, ask for detailed and concrete information on the practical implications of this provision.

Tax regime: this is a point you must always check because life assurance is not always a deductible tax allowance if concluded with a foreign firm.

React rapidly: what if, despite your vigilance, you have not received the documents you want? Have you been burgled and not yet been compensated? Do you have to wait too long for payment? Or has the insurer invoked exemptions not foreseen in your contract? Quick! Contact your consumer association, your cross-border European consumer information centre and/or your national inspection authority!

Beware of aggressive selling techniques: certain insurance

companies practice telephone selling to woo nationals of Member States in which they are not established. Since this activity falls within the scope of the freedom to provide services, the company concerned must prove that it is entitled, under its licensing arrangements, to insure private risks. But pay attention: this 'direct line' selling technique, which is widely utilized by German, British and Netherlands companies, is not regulated at Community level (see Chapter 5 on canvassing and Chapter 6 on distance selling). Hence the need, for the moment, to be vigilant when you are invited to take out a policy in another country of the European Union.

What remains to be done

Rules for compensating victims still differ from one country to another, and each country has its own patent remedies for determining liability or assessing risks in the event of an accident. Since the law applicable is that of the country in which the accident occurred, the damages you receive will depend very much on local rules.

With regard to fire insurance, the problem is that Community rules in no way oblige your insurer to communicate detailed particulars concerning the content and scope of the commitment you have entered into!

Specific sectors

And finally ...

 If I'm not mistaken, we still have quite a way to go before the single market is fully operational for consumers.

That's right. Just as the job of building Europe in general is a never-ending process, completion of the single market is a **long-term affair,** as you may have observed in reading this guide.

Substantial progress has been achieved over the years, albeit gradually, and so everyday life in the European market has not been revolutionized overnight.

However, the lure of protectionism is still present when it comes to surreptitiously raising obstacles to the free movement of persons, goods, services and capital. To accomplish what remains to be done and to stamp out protectionism, which in the long run always hurts the consumer, consumers must play **an active role** in building the European Union.

 I don't see how my behaviour can change anything.

Wrong. **You too have a role to play** in ensuring that the single market works to your advantage. In your everyday life:

■ get information and compare offers, particularly when planning a major outlay;

■ regularly check your purchases. (Are the products safe? Do they correspond to your expectations?);

Specific sectors

- in the event of dissatisfaction, take action: tell your acquaintances what has happened, notify the competent authorities, a consumer association and/or the press;

- above all, stand up for your rights!

Remember that the market is like a democracy: whenever you buy a good or service you are in a manner of speaking voting with your pocket. So **choose the best candidates!**

 What should I do in the event of a problem?

The first thing is to **complain** to the service provider, the manufacturer or the dealer, as the case may be. Remember that as a consumer **you have rights** that are summarized in this guide.

You have not received satisfaction? Then move up a gear: **take your complaint to the appropriate local, regional or national organization:** consumer organizations, arbitration boards responsible for the domain in question, business watchdog or anti-fraud agencies — it is quite easy to find somebody to talk to. In most cases even a telephone call will help put you in the picture.

When your question or problem has **cross-border aspects** (supplier established in a neighbouring country, product purchased abroad, etc.), you can also contact one of the **European cross-border consumer information centres (see Chapter 3 on information, advice and access to justice). Their staff are experts in the field of European consumer law. Moreover, that way you can be sure that your 'case' will be heard by the European Commission, which will thus garner information on sectors where the single market has not yet achieved all its objectives.**

 What are the current priorities of the European Union in consumer affairs?

The three-year action plan adopted by the European

Commission in 1993 targeted 'placing the single market at the service of European consumers'. This plan of action focuses on three major strands:

- consolidation of existing legislation;

- more information for consumers;

- better access to justice.

Other priorities include greater transparency in cross-border payments, improved guarantee and after-sales service conditions, a legal framework for distance selling, and the introduction of the European eco-label for staple consumer goods.

Hence, European consumers can anticipate steady improvements in the years to come.

 I wasn't aware that the European Union was so concerned about my daily life

Perhaps this guide has helped you see things from a different angle. Now you know that Europe is not a 'machine' remote from people's daily cares. On the contrary: **the European Union puts people first**. Very often, people are not aware that the decisions taken by the national governments are based on decisions **taken jointly by the 15 Member States, with the support of the European Parliament which you have directly elected.**

If in future **'Europe of the consumer'** means more to you than just a slogan, this guide will have achieved its objective.

Europe of the consumer:
Europe at your service

Specific sectors

Annexes

Useful addresses

The European Commission

■ European Commission
Directorate-General XXIV — Consumer Policy
Rue de la Loi 200
B-1049 Brussels
Tel. (32-2) 299 11 11
Fax (32-2) 296 32 79

European and interregional organizations

At European level, the following five organizations, each covering a specific field, are concerned with consumer issues and contribute to the development of the European Union's consumer policy:

European Bureau of Consumers' Unions (BEUC)
Avenue de Tervuren 36, boîte 4
B-1040 Brussels
Tel. (32-2) 735 31 10
Fax (32-2) 735 74 55

European Confederation of Consumers' Cooperatives (Eurocoop)
Rue Archimède 17, boîte 2
B-1040 Brussels
Tel. (32-2) 285 00 70
Fax (32-2) 231 07 57

European Trade Union Confederation (ETUC)
Boulevard Émile Jacqmain 155
B-1210 Brussels
Tel. (32-2) 224 05 40
Fax (32-2) 224 05 41

Confederation of Family Organizations in the EC (Coface)
Rue de Londres 17
B-1050 Brussels
Tel. (32-2) 511 41 79
Fax (32-2) 514 47 73

European Interregional Institute of Consumer Affairs (IEIC)
79, rue Gantois
F-59000 Lille
Tel. (33-20) 21 92 50
Fax (33-20) 54 18 45

National organizations

In several countries, the most popular consumer advocacy groups operate at regional or even local level. But since this guide is only intended as an introduction, the directory is limited to organizations at European or national level. In most cases these organizations can give you the addresses of the info-points or advice centres best equipped to deal with your questions or problems. In each country, the first address mentioned (in a box) is that of the central government ministry responsible for consumer protection legislation.

The Commission is currently drawing up a much more comprehensive list of all non-commercial consumer organizations. The organizations listed in the following pages will be informed as soon as this overview has become available.

Remember: The organizations listed in this directory are not the only ones to deal with consumer questions. There are also organizations (both commercial and non-commercial) which have other, more specific roles and skills (for example, automobile clubs) and can thus provide consumers with extremely valuable information and services. Unfortunately, we do not have space to include them here.

■ Belgium

Ministère des Affaires économiques/
Ministerie van Economische Zaken
Service 'Consommation'/dienst Verbruik
N.G. III
Boulevard Émile Jacqmain/Émile Jacqmainlaan 154
B-1210 Bruxelles/Brussel
Tel. (32-2) 206 41 11
Fax (32-2) 206 57 71

Centre de recherche et d'information des consommateurs/
Onderzoeks en Informatiecentrum van de Verbruikersorganisaties (CRIOC)
Rue des Chevaliers/Ridderstraat 28
B-1050 Bruxelles/Brussel
Tel. (32-2) 547 06 11
Fax (32-2) 547 06 01

Association des consommateurs `test-achats'/
Verbruikersunie 'Test Aankoop'
Rue de Hollande /Hollandstraat 13
B-1060 Bruxelles/Brussel
Tel. (32-2) 542 32 11
Fax (32-2) 542 32 50

Conseil de la consommation/
Raad voor het Verbruik
Boulevard Émile Jacqmain/Émile Jacqmainlaan 154
B-1210-Bruxelles/Brussel
Tel. (32-2) 206 41 11
Fax (32-2) 206 57 52

■ Denmark

Erhvervsministeriet (Ministry of Industry)
Slotsholmsgade 10-12
DK-1216 København K
Tel. (45) 33 92 33 50
Fax (45) 33 12 37 78

Forbrugerrådet
Fiolstræde 17
PO Box 2188
DK-1017 København K
Tel. (45) 33 13 63 11
Fax (45) 33 13 41 15

Forbrugerstyrelsen
Amagerfælledvej 56
DK-2300 København S
Tel. (45) 31 57 01 00
Fax (45) 32 96 02 32

Nordisk Ministerråd
Nordisk Embedsmandskomite for Forbrugerspørgsmål
Store Strandstræde 18
DK-1255 København K
Tel. (45) 33 96 02 00
Fax (45) 33 96 02 02

■ Germany

Ministerium für Wirtschaft
Villemomblerstraße 76
D-53107 Bonn
Tel. (49-228) 61 50 00
Fax (49-228) 615 44 36

In Germany, the consumer information and advisory services (*Verbraucherzentralen*) are organized on a *Land* (or State) basis. If you want to know the addresses of the offices in each *Land,* contact the headquarters (AGV) at the following address:

Arbeitsgemeinschaft der Verbraucherverbände (AGV)
Heilsbachstraße 20
D-53123 Bonn
Tel. (49-228) 648 90
Fax (49-228) 64 42 58

Stiftung Warentest
Lützowplatz 11-13
D-10785 Berlin
Tel. (49-30) 263 10
Fax (49-30) 263 14 28

■ **Greece**

Ipourgeion Emporiou (Ministry of Commerce)
Kaningos Square
GR-10181 Athina
Tel. (30-1) 381 62 41-50 (main switchboard)
(30-1) 382 16 18 or 384 17 73
(Consumer Protection and Information Section)
Fax (30-1) 384 26 42

Ekpizo (Quality of life)
Valtetsiou 43-45
GR-10681 Athens
Tel (30-1) 330 06 73
Fax (30-1) 330 05 91

KEPKA (Consumer Protection Centre)
Vas. Irakliou 40
GR-54623 Thessaloniki
Tel. (30-31) 269 449
Fax (30-31) 242 211 or 252 362

INKA (Consumers' Institute)
Leof. Poseidonos 31
GR-17561 Pal. Faliro
Tel. (30-1) 982 91 52
Fax (30-1) 982 50 96

■ Spain

Ministerio de Sanidad y Consumo
Paseo del Prado 18-20
E-28071 Madrid
Tel. (34-1) 420 00 00
Fax (34-1) 420 12 92

Information and protection of consumers is mainly the responsibility of the different provinces. Moreover, in most major cities you will find the municipal consumer information offices (OMIC). If there is no such office close to you, you can always contact the Instituto Nacional del Consumo at the following address:

Instituto Nacional del Consumo (INC)
C/Príncipe de Vergara 54
E-28006 Madrid
Tel. (34-1) 431 18 36
Fax (34-1) 576 39 27

Confederación Estatal de Consumidores y Usuarios (CECU)
C/Cava Baja 30
E-28005 Madrid
Tel. (34-1) 364 02 76/364 05 22
Fax (34-1) 366 90 00

Eroski, S. Coop
Bº San Augustín s/n
E-48230 Elorrio (Bizkaia)/Vizcaya
Tel. (34-4) 658 24 11
Fax (34-4) 682 12 26

Confederación Española de Asociaciones de Amas de Casa, Consumidores y Usuarios (Ceaccu)
Paseo de la Castellana 113, 4º Dcha
E-28046 Madrid
Tel. (34-1) 555 58 11
Fax (34-1) 597 24 50

Organización de Consumidores y Usuarios (OCU)
C/Milán 38
E-28043 Madrid
Tel. (34-1) 300 00 45
Fax (34-1) 388 73 72

Unión de Consumidores de España (UCE)
Atocha 26, 3° Izda
E-28012 Madrid
Tel. (34-1) 369 13 76 or 369 14 12
Fax (34-1) 429 66 06

■ **France**

Ministère de l'Économie
59, boulevard Vincent-Auriol
F-75703 Paris Cedex 13
Tel. (33-1) 44 87 17 17
Fax (33-1) 44 97 33 66

Consumer assistance in France is decentralized: you will find the centres techniques régionaux de la consommation (CTRC) in all regions, while each *département* has its own *direction départementale de la consommation, de la concurrence et de la répression des fraudes (DDCCRF)*. Moreover, many municipalities have consumer standby advice and information services run by consumer organizations.

Institut national de la consommation (INC)
80, rue Lecourbe
F-75732 Paris Cedex 15
Tel. (33-1) 45 66 20 20
Fax (33-1) 45 66 21 50

DDCCRF (bureau central)
Carré Diderot
315, boulevard Diderot
F-75572 Paris Cedex 11
Tel. (33-1) 44 87 27 00
Fax (33-1) 44 87 30 42

Twenty consumer organizations have been officially recognized at national level as representing consumers and defending their interests:

Association d'éducation et d'information des consommateurs de la fédération d'éducation nationale (ADEIC FEN)
3, rue de la Rochefoucauld
F-75009 Paris
Tel. (33-1) 44 53 73 93
Fax (33-1) 44 53 73 94

Association Force Ouvrière 'Consommateurs' (AFOC)
141, avenue du Maine
F-75014 Paris
Tel. (33-1) 30 52 85 85
Fax (33-1) 30 52 85 86

Association fédérale des nouveaux consommateurs (ANC)
31bis, avenue du Maréchal-de-Lattre-de-Tassigny
F-94220 Charenton
Tel. (33-1) 45 18 06 00
Fax (33-1) 42 18 52 91

Association 'étude et consommation' Confédération française démocratique du travail (Asseco CFDT)
4, boulevard de la Villette
F-75019 Paris
Tel. (33-1) 42 03 83 50
Fax (33-1) 42 03 81 45

Confédération générale du logement (CGL)
143-147, boulevard Anatole France
F-93285 Saint-Denis Cedex
Tel. (33-1) 48 09 37 41
Fax (33-1) 48 09 08 96

Conseil national des associations de familles laïques (CNAFAL)
108, avenue Ledru-Rollin
F-75011 Paris
Tel. (33-1) 47 00 03 40
Fax (33-1) 47 00 01 86

Confédération nationale des associations de familles catholiques (CNAFC)
28, place Saint-Georges
F-75009 Paris
Tel. (33-1) 48 78 81 61
Fax (33-1) 48 78 07 35

CNAPFS
1, rue de Maubeuge
F-75009 Paris
Tel. (33-1) 42 80 27 05
Fax (33-1) 45 26 24 63

Confédération nationale du logement (CNL)
8, rue Mériel
BP 119
F-93104 Montreuil Cedex
Tel. (33-1) 48 57 04 64
Fax (33-1) 48 57 73 30

Confédération syndicale du cadre de vie (CSCV)
15, place d'Aligre
F-75012 Paris
Tel. (33-1) 53 17 17 15
Fax (33-1) 43 41 40 06

Confédération syndicale des familles (CSF)
53, rue Riquet
F-75019 Paris
Tel. (33-1) 44 89 86 80
Fax (33-1) 40 35 29 52

Familles rurales
81, avenue Raymond Poincaré
F-75116 Paris
Tel. (33-1) 47 04 94 63
Fax (33-1) 47 27 32 47

Familles de France (FF)
28, place Saint-Georges
F-75009 Paris
Tel. (33-1) 44 53 45 90
Fax (33-1) 45 53 17 56

Fédération nationale des associations d'usagers des transports (FNAUT)
32, rue Raymond Losserand
F-75014 Paris
Tel. (33-1) 43 35 02 83
Fax (33-1) 43 35 14 06

Association pour l'information et la défense des consommateurs salariés — Confédération générale du travail (Indecosa CGT)
263, rue de Paris
F-93516 Montreuil Cedex
Tel. (33-1) 48 18 84 26
Fax (33-1) 48 18 84 82

Fédération nationale Léo Lagrange (FNLL)
12, cité Malesherbes
F-75009 Paris
Tel. (33-1) 44 53 30 80
Fax (33-1) 44 53 30 85

Organisation générale des consommateurs (Orgeco)
43, rue Marx Dormoy
F-75018 Paris
Tel. (33-1) 46 07 09 65
Fax (33-1) 46 07 06 83

Union fédérale des consommateurs (UFC, Que choisir?)
11, rue Guénot
F-75011 Paris Cedex 11
Tel. (33-1) 43 48 95 55
Fax (33-1) 43 48 24 76

Union féminine civique et sociale (UFCS)
6, rue Béranger
F-75003 Paris
Tel. (33-1) 44 54 50 54
Fax (33-1) 44 54 50 66

Union nationale des associations familiales (UNAF)
28, place Saint-Georges
F-75009 Paris
Tel. (33-1) 49 95 36 00
Fax (33-1) 40 16 12 76

■ **Ireland**

Department of Enterprise and Employment
Setanta Centre
South Great Frederick Street
Dublin 2, Ireland
Tel. (353-1) 661 44 44
Fax (353-1) 676 26 54

Office of Consumer Affairs & Fair Trade
Shelbourne House
Shelbourne Road
Dublin 2, Ireland
Tel. (353-1) 661 33 99
Fax (353-1) 660 67 63

Consumers' Association of Ireland
45 Upper Mount Street
Dublin 2, Ireland
Tel. (353-1) 661 24 66
Fax (353-1) 661 24 64

■ **Italy**

Ministero dell'industria del commercio e dell'artigianato
Direzione generale del commercio interno e dei consumi
industriali
Divisione III—Tutela dei consumatori
Via Molise 2
I-00187 Roma
Tel. (39-6) 481 49 46
Fax (39-6) 488 53 96

The consumer organizations listed below have regional or
local branches.

Associazione italiana difesa consumatori e ambiente (Adiconsum)
Via G.N. Lancisi 25
I-00161 Roma
Tel. (39-6) 441 70 21
Fax (39-6) 441 70 230

Associazione per la difesa é l'orientamento dei consumatori (ADOC)
Via Lucullo 6
I-00187 Roma
Tel. (39-6) 482 58 49
Fax (39-6) 481 90 28

Adusbef (utenti bancari)
Via Farini 62
I-00185 Roma
Tel. (39-6) 481 86 32
Fax (39-6) 481 86 33

Assoconsumatori
Via Rabirio 1
I-00196 Roma
Tel. (39-6) 578 23 92
Fax (39-6) 575 83 585

Associazione consumatori e utenti (ex Agrisalus)
Via Bazzini 4
I-20131 Milano
Tel. (39-2) 706 306 68
Fax (39-2) 266 806 64

Assoutenti
Via Celimontana 38
I-00186 Roma
Tel. (39-6) 704 505 94
Fax (39-6) 700 15 71

Codacons
Viale Mazzini 73
I-00195 Roma
Tel. (39-6) 325 17 38
Fax (39-6) 325 24 50

Comitato difesa consumatori
Via della Liberazione 18
I-20124 Milano
Tel. (**39-2**) 667 204 10
Fax (**39-2**) 670 63 80

Federconsumatori
Via Goito 39
I-00185 Roma
Tel. (39-6) 49 00 81
Fax (39-6) 49 00 89

Lega consumatori ACLI
Via delle Orchidee 4
I-20100 Milano
Tel. (39-2) 483 036 59
Fax (39-2) 483 026 11

Movimento consumatori (ARCI)
Via Adige 11
I-20135 Milano
Tel. (39-2) 545 65 51
Fax (39-2) 546 65 00

Movimento difesa cittadino
Via Gregoriana 5
I-00187 Roma
Tel. (39-6) 699 425 12
Fax (39-6) 699 425 13

Movimento federativo democratico
Via F. de Sanctis 15
I-00195 Roma
Tel. (39-6) 372 27 04
Fax (39-6) 372 27 26

Unione nazionale consumatori (UNC)
Via Andrea Doria 48
I-00192 Roma
Tel. (39-6) 397 370 21/2
Fax (39-6) 397 333 29

■ **Luxembourg**

Ministère de l'Économie
19-21, boulevard Royal
L-2914 Luxembourg
Tel. (352) 478 41 37
Fax (352) 46 04 48

Ministère des Classes moyennes et du Tourisme
6, avenue Emile Reuter
L-2937 Luxembourg
Tel. (352) 478 47 13
Fax (352) 478 47 40

Ministère de la Famille et de la Solidarité
12-14, avenue Emile Reuter
L-2919 Luxembourg
Tel. (352) 478 47 81
Fax (352) 478 65 70

Union luxembourgeoise des consommateurs (ULC)
55, rue des Bruyères
L-1274 Howald
Tel. (352) 49 60 22
Fax (352) 49 49 57

■ **The Netherlands**

Ministerie van Economische Zaken
Directie Marktwerking
Afdeling Algemeen Marktbeleid
Postbus 20101
NL-2500 EC Den Haag
Tel. (31-70) 379 79 95
Fax (31-70) 379 73 40

Consumentenbond
Postbus 1000
NL-2500 BA Den Haag
Tel. (31-70) 445 45 45
Fax (31-70) 445 45 90

SWOKA
Alexanderstraat 14
NL-2514 JL Den Haag
Tel. (31-70) 346 92 25
Fax (31-70) 360 39 63

■ **Austria**

Bundesministerium für Gesundheit und Konsumenten-schutz
Gruppe Konsumentenschutz
Radetzkystraße 2
A-1030 Wien
Tel. (43-1) 711 72 47 75/47 85
Fax (43-1) 715 58 31

Verein für Konsumenteninformation (VKI)
Mariahilferstraße 81
A-1060 Wien
Tel. (43-1) 587 86 86
Fax (43-1) 587 93 00

VKI branch offices are located in Steiermark, Tyrol,
Oberösterreich and Burgenland.

Bundesarbeitskammer
Prinz-Eugen-Straße 20-22
A-1040 Wien
Tel. (43-1) 501 65
Fax (43-1) 501 65 22 30

■ Portugal

Inspecção-Geral das Actividades Económicas
Avenida Duque de Ávila, 139
P-1150 Lisboa
Tel. (351-1) 356 01 01
Fax (351-1) 353 36 86 or 54 01 40

Instituto do Consumidor
Praça Duque de Saldanha, 31-3°
P-1000 Lisboa
Tel. (351-1) 54 40 25
Fax (351-1) 52 24 10

Associação Portuguesa para a Defesa do Consumidor (DECO)
Avenida dos Defensores de Chaves, 22-1°
P-1000 Lisboa
Tel. (351-1) 57 39 08
Fax (351-1) 57 78 51

■ Finland

Kauppa- ja teollisuusministeriö (Ministry of Trade and Industry)
PO Box 230
Aleksanderinkatu 4
FIN-00171 Helsinki
Tel. (358-0) 1601
Fax (358-0) 160 2670

Kuluttajavirasto (National Consumer Office)
PO Box 403
Haapaniemenkatu 4
FIN-00531 Helsinki
Tel. (358-0) 77261
Fax (358-0) 7726 7557

Kuluttaja-Asiamies/Konsument Ombudsman (Consumer Ombudsman) and Kuluttajavalituslautakunta/Konsumentklagonämnden (Consumer Complaints Commission)
PO Box 306
Kaikukatu 3
FIN-00531 Helsinki
Tel. (358-0) 7 72 61
Fax (358-0) 753 0357

Suomen Kuluttajaliitto
Mannerheimintie 15A
FIN-00260 Helsinki
Tel. (358-0) 448 288 959
Fax (358-0) 448 725

Kuluttajat — Konsumenterna
Vilhonkatu 6 F 31
FIN-00100 Helsinki
Tel. (358-0) 626 206
(No fax)

Marttaliitto — Martha Förbund
Uudenmaankatu 24A
FIN-00120 Helsinki
Tel. (358-0) 646 217
Fax (358-0) 680 1266

■ **Sweden**

Civildepartementet
S-103 33 Stockholm
Tel. (46-8) 405 10 00
Fax (46-8) 791 78 99

Konsumentverket
Box 503
S-162 15 Vällingby
Tel. (46-8) 759 83 00
Fax (46-8) 38 22 15

Sveriges Konsumentråd
PO Box 20063
S-104 60 Stockholm
Tel. (46-8) 772 89 68
Fax (46-8) 642 81 06

Konsumenter i Samverkan
PO Box 88
S-57722 Hultsfred
Tel. (46-495) 413 15
Fax (46-495) 413 15

■ United Kingdom

Department of Trade and Industry
Consumer Affairs Division
Victoria Street
London SW1 0ET, United Kingdom
Tel. (44-171) 215 50 00
Fax (44-171) 222 92 80

Office of Fair Trading
Consumer Affairs Division
Field House
Bream's Buildings
London EC4A 1PR, United Kingdom
Tel. (44-171) 242 28 58
Fax (44-171) 268 88 00

National Consumer Council
20 Grosvenor Gardens
London SW1W 0DH, United Kingdom
Tel. (44-171) 730 34 69
Fax (44-171) 730 01 91

Consumers' Association
2 Marylebone Road
London NW1 4DF, United Kingdom
Tel. (44-171) 830 60 00
Fax (44-171) 830 62 20

Consumers in Europe Group (CEG)
24 Tufton Street
London SW1P 3RB, United Kingdom
Tel. (44-171) 222 26 62
Fax (44-171) 222 85 86

In most cities you will find Citizens Advice Bureaux. If you cannot find a bureau close to you, contact the National Association of Citizens Advice Bureaux at the address given below:

National Association of Citizens Advice Bureaux
115-123 Pentonville Road
London N1 9LZ, United Kingdom
Tel. (44-171) 833 21 81
Fax (44-171) 833 43 71

The institutions and legislation of the European Union

This annex gives a brief overview of the institutions of the European Union. For further details, readers may consult a Commission publication entitled *'The Institutions of the European Community'* (Europe dossier No 8/91) which can be obtained from:

■ Office for Official Publications
of the European Communities
L-2985 Luxembourg.

All the official publications can also be obtained from the Commission representations in the Member States. You will find them listed in the telephone book.

Below you will find a brief description of the composition and role of the various Community institutions, as well as the two consultative bodies: the Economic and Social Committee and the Committee of the Regions.

A — Community institutions

Following the enlargement of the European Union to include Austria, Finland and Sweden, the institutions have the following composition.

The Council of Ministers

The Council of Ministers is the main decision-making body

of the European Union. It is made up of the ministers responsible for the domains in question in each Member State.

In recent years the Council of Ministers responsible for consumer protection has met on average twice a year, but certain decisions with potential implications for consumers have been taken by other councils, for example those dealing with the internal market, economics and finance, agriculture and the budget.

The Commission

As of 1995 the Commission will consist of 20 members nominated by common consent by the 15 Member States for a period of five years. The main roles of the Commission are as follows:

■ as guardian of the Treaties, it monitors the implementation of Community law;

■ it issues proposals on Community policy and legislation;

■ it manages certain policies (for example the customs union, the common agricultural policy);

■ it takes decisions in certain domains such as competition policy.

The European Parliament

The European Parliament consists of 626 MEPs elected every five years by direct universal suffrage. Its main role is consultation and supervision, but since 1993 in certain cases it enjoys codecision powers with the Council of Ministers.

The detailed examination of Commission proposals is the job of specialized Parliamentary committees. Proposals relating to consumer affairs are dealt with by the Committee for the Environment, Public Health and Consumer Protection.

The Court of Justice

The Court of Justice is made up of 15 judges and seven advocates-general, who are appointed by common agreement between the Member States for a six-year period; every three years, seven (or eight) judges and three (or four) advocates-general are replaced or their term of office is renewed.

The role of the Court of Justice is to interpret and apply Community legislation. The Court of Justice also rules on complaints concerning Community legislation and decisions taken by the other Community institutions.

The Court of Justice is assisted by a Court of First Instance, made up of 15 judges, which mainly deals with competition matters.

The Court of Auditors

The Court of Auditors is the fifth institution following the entry into effect of the Treaty on European Union and consists of a representative of each Member State. It is responsible for auditing expenditure under the Community budget.

B — Consultative bodies

The Economic and Social Committee

The Economic and Social Committee (ESC) consists of 222 representatives of various categories of persons involved in the social and economic life of the European Union, as regards employers, workers and other interest groups such as consumers.

The Economic and Social Committee has a consultative role — it must be consulted in certain cases and may be consulted in others. It may also deliver opinions on its own initiative.

The Committee of the Regions

Established by the Treaty on European Union, this consultative body ensures that the voice of the regions and local authorities is always heard in connection with decision-making procedures. Its 222 members, from all parts of Europe, can now for the first time deliver opinions on all draft laws relating to the regions (for example, concerning infrastructure).

C — Community legislation

Types of Community legislation

Pursuant to the Treaties, the institutions of the European Union may:

- adopt regulations,

- adopt directives,

- take decisions,

- formulate recommendations, or

- formulate opinions.

Regulations do not have to be ratified by the national parliaments to have binding effect. In the event of conflict between a regulation and existing national law, the regulation prevails.

Directives, most of which are adopted by Council and Parliament, bind the Member States as to the results to be achieved within a given period, but leave it open to the national governments to choose how to implement them. As such a directive does not have legal effect in the Member States, but its particular provisions **may** have direct effect if the directive is not duly transposed.

Decisions are specific to their addressees, in respect of which they are mandatory in all their elements, with regard to Member States, firms and private individuals. Decisions imposing financial obligations are enforceable by the national courts.

Recommendations and **opinions** do not have binding effect; they simply reflect the opinion of the institution that issues them.

Update
February 1996

Since the manuscript was drafted the following major developments have taken place:

Chapter 3: Information, advice and access to justice

You are no longer all alone!

The Commission adopted in January 1996 a proposal for legislation which greatly improves the possibilities for consumers to deal with cross-border disputes with retailers or manufacturers. The proposal sets minimum conditions for the **mutual recognition of consumer organizations and/or other competent bodies to act in the general interest of consumers (but not on behalf of individual consumers) in countries of the Union other than their home country:** if consumers in country A are victims of a practice originating in country B, and which is unlawful according to Community consumer law, these recognized bodies will be able to intervene in country B on behalf of these consumers, either directly or via their equivalents in country B, to prevent this.

The proposal will now go to the Council and the European Parliament for decision; this process may result in changes to the original proposal.

Two new cross-border information centres

Two new centres have opened: Bolzano for the Austro-Italian border region (late 1995) and Dublin for Ireland, Northern Ireland and hence the UK (spring 1996).

Bolzano:
Via Dodiciville, 11
I–Bolzano
Tel. (39 471)97 68 23/98 09 39
Fax (39 471)97 99 14

Dublin:
European Consumer Information Centre
Provisional address:
4/5 Harcourt Road
Dublin 2
Ireland
Tel. (353 1)661 33 99
Fax (353 1)660 67 63

Chapter 9: Labelling

Unit prices

The Commission has proposed legislation according to which **not only the selling price but also the unit price** must normally be indicated; the Council and the European Parliament have yet to approve the proposal.

Chapter 10: Labelling and food and drink

Language on food labels

The current position, likely to be finally confirmed by the summer of 1996, is that the information to be found on food labels must be in **a language easily understood** by consumers, provided they are not informed by other means (photos, pictogrammes, diagrams, etc.); furthermore, labelling may be in more than one language.

The practical consequence of this is that Member States may insist on labelling in their national language(s), but they may not forbid labelling in other languages or by other means.

There are currently **no plans to propose general legislation** on the use of languages in labelling.

Food and drink:

Additives

Legislation on sweeteners, colouring agents and other food additives has entered into force at the end of 1995 or will come into force in July and September 1996. In summary, this legislation accepts **a wider use of additives than in the past, but the use is circumscribed in strict rules:**

- only additives listed in the legislation may be used;

- the composition of the recognized additives is defined in detail in the legislation, to protect the health and safety of consumers.

Chapter 16: Travel and tourism

The Schengen Agreement

The Schengen Agreement includes a **safeguard clause** permitting the re-introduction of controls at the frontiers for reasons of public order. This clause has been invoked by **France**; the situation is, however, under constant surveillance.

Finally, **a precision** (which is clear in some language versions of the guide but not in others):

It is not only the citizens of Ireland, Denmark, Sweden and Finland who are subject to the restrictions in purchases of alcohol and/or tobacco products mentioned on page 25, but all travellers entering these countries.

European Commission

European consumer guide to the single market: Second edition

Luxembourg: Office for Official Publications of the European Communities

1996 — 229 pp. — 14.8 x 21 cm

ISBN 92-827-4859-6

Price (excluding VAT) in Luxembourg: ECU 9